REVIEWS FOR GEMS

Dr. Toni Kleckley is challenging a generation of seasoned women to preserve a legacy, which has the potential for being lost, by providing them with the tools to tap into the curiosity and desire of a younger generation of women to know about and understand the importance of the accomplishments of past generations and how these can shape their future."

— BARBARA TURPIN, OHIO GRANDPARENT KINSHIP COALITION

Grandmothers Educating Minds (GEMS) was a refreshing and much-needed read. Our future generations are missing out on some of the key elements that were highlighted in this book. I could relate to such things as; having a grandmother that shared our family history and the accomplishments of some of my late relatives. Grandmothers and their wisdom are an undervalued treasure in the time that we live in now. I appreciate the authors' use of scripture which gives the foundation of the role of a grandmother. The bonus to this book was the interactive journal pages that encourage the reader to take time and process and reflect on what they have read. GEMS is a book that our young people need, and I am so glad that Toni has taken the time and written it.

— KELLIE BOLTON

This book will be a very useful, informative, and helpful tool for those seeking to understand relative caregiving.

— RONALD R. BROWDER EXECUTIVE CONSULTANT FOR THE OHIO FEDERATION FOR HEALTH EQUITY AND SOCIAL JUSTICE

I loved the preview! I especially like that you have given actionable items so the information is reinforced.

Keep up this great work. One thing I regret is not getting the stories and wisdom from our grandparents and their generation before they passed on.

— CRYSTAL BRANNER

This is an excellent book, easy to read, and at a level for everyone to be able to understand— from college level to grade school. This book is excellent. I am so proud of you, my little sis.

— GLORIA KENLEY

This is beautifully written, Soror Kleckley.

— CHARITY MARTIN-KING, PRES; GAMMA ZETA ZETA CHAPTER

GRANDMOTHERS EDUCATING MINDS, 2ND EDITION

GRANDMOTHERS EDUCATING MINDS, 2ND EDITION

THE LEGACY AND MENTORSHIP OF THE SEASONED WOMAN

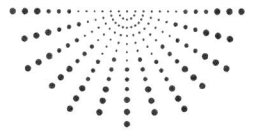

TONI KLECKLEY, TH.D.

J Merrill Publishing, Inc.
434 Hillpine Drive
Columbus, OH 43207
www.JMerrill.pub

Library of Congress Control Number: 2021917820
ISBN-13: 978-1-954414-21-1 (Paperback)
ISBN-13: 978-1-954414-20-4 (eBook)

Book Title: Grandmothers Educating Minds, 2nd Edition
Author: Toni Kleckley
Editing: Dennis Brown
Cover Artwork: Khia Ancalade

To God:

Thank You for the daily blessings, Your love, and Your mercy. I am truly humbled that You have entrusted me with the vision and the insights that have come together in this book. And I now offer to you the gift you gave to me. I seek Your anointing on the words it contains as well as those who read them.

To my husband, Mathis:

I am eternally grateful for you. Our hearts are intertwined with Christ. I appreciate all your prayers, your patience, and your encouragement.

To my awesome parents, Raymond and Joan:

Thank you for your unwavering love, your undeniable faith, and your selfless support. Thanks for passing your wisdom to me.

To my two amazing children Ta'Nia and Wesley:

I could not be prouder. You're my heart with wings. Continue to fly.

To my six marvelous grandchildren, Ja'Vonte, Ta'Yonna, Da'Veon, Ja'Leyah, Gabriel, and Wesley Jr.

A personal note to my grandchildren: Each of us is a unique and special gift from God that I cherish.

When I started to write this book, it was with you in mind. I wanted to give you the knowledge and be blessed by my grandmother – your great-great-

grandmother – whom you didn't get to know. She was a fine lady with the depth of wisdom and valuable lessons.

This book is designed to help you determine who is the right person or group of people who mean you well and who you will allow in your lives.

Another reason for leaving you this book is your great-great-grandmother became afflicted with dementia that later developed into Alzheimer's. It is a genetic disease that is very debilitating. I watched her slowly wither away and disappear into the foggy emptiness of lost memories. I felt my own emptiness as she no longer recognized those of us who had loved and who had loved her. She no longer remembers the hugs, tears, words of wisdom, or powerful prayer we shared throughout the years. Alzheimer's sinister effects robbed her of what she held dear.

So, as I recall and reflect on my time with Mimi and all that she shared with me, I choose to share those memories and our history with you, my grandchildren.

My precious darlings, I love each one of you forever. My grandmother was a GEM, and she still shines in my heart. Remember to pass your own stories forward and help others discover their greatness, as I am doing with you today.

You will always have a piece of me on these pages.

Love,
Mommy Toni, Your GEM

And now a very special dedication to my Grandmother "Mimi:"
I will always cherish my memories of you and consider it a sacred honor to share those memories with others. Your life is the inspiration behind this book, and I dedicate it to you. You may have missed out on the red-carpet treatment here, but your feet know the joy of walking the heavenly streets of Gold.

Finally, to all those who read this book and get a glimpse of the calling that shone so vividly through my grandmother's life:

May these pages spur you on in your pursuit of becoming the GEM God longs for you to be.

ACKNOWLEDGMENTS

To the "GEMs" and seasoned women, the "Grands" who were instrumental in guiding me through the maze of life, the innovative, idealistic women who believed in me. They opened my eyes and mind showing me I could do anything or become anyone I wanted, helping me embrace challenges without fearing a new experience.

To my mother, who educates the minds of her grandchildren and great-grandchildren. She was a Licensed Practical Nurse serving compassionately for thirty-six years and remains a person that faithfully reflects dedication and devotion for people. Thank you for being my prayer partner, best friend, and confidant. Your family loves your strength and honors you.

I will always cherish the work of teachers. They helped position me from my youth and set me on a positive career course. So many memories have worked hand-in-hand, affecting how I matured into the woman I am today.

In remembrance of Ms. Alice Huddleston, my amazing elementary teacher, who died at eighty-four. She set high expectations for me academically. I always felt she cared.

Ms. Gloria Jones, who taught in the elementary school system. Her mentorship inspired me to be creative through the arts, which gave me confidence in my first ballet recital.

In remembrance of Ms. Louise T. Batties, my high school teacher, who was also a distinguished role model and mentor. She was also extremely passionate about the education of youth. She would passionately correct me when I used the words, "I can't."

Thank all those who contributed to the success of the physical creation to the completion of my book: Jackie Merrill and J Merrill Publishing Team.

To Ms. Sharina LaShawn, thanks for your assistance in the first edition and taking time to assemble my disorganized puzzle of notes and for making sense of them.

Finally, to Jeannette M. Jarrett, second editor and a referee, I gratefully acknowledge her unwavering stamina to help, making everything flow over the months. You're the best!!!

Representatives of Legacy,
A medley of ageless songs
We are pages in a book
We are stories to be read
Chronicle throughout history
We are here

Timeless, Stately, Heartwarming,
Housing a Repertoire of skills
We are Role Models
Epitomized, Excellent and Mosaic
We are here

We are famous, illustrated, and passionate,
We are believers, demonstrators, expeditors,
We make the impossible, possible
We are talented messengers
Carriers of life
Dreamers, accomplishers, achievers, dependable
Successors, benefactors, decedents
We are here

Guardians, Protectors, Defenders, Cheerleaders and Coaches
Proud, Gentle, soft but resilient
Tall in our struts
Shoulders back
Proper in speech
Vigilant, Watchful and Effective
We are here

Arm to Arm
Face to Face
Color to Color
Our presence screams in the atmosphere
We are not connected by high heels, lipstick, mops and brooms
We are united by being born a girl
Unchained, Dignified, Respectful
Free to be me
We are here

Creators, duplicators, but not imitators
Deifying the odds
Edifying our spirit
Unify by our nature
Champions by choice
Inductees in the Hall of GEMs
We are here.

— AUTHOR TONI KLECKLEY

Before another word:

"What is a GEM?"

A GEM:

A Woman whose life, wisdom, and passion have served to mold and inspire the hearts and minds of the generations of young people in her pathway.

She is a seasoned, mature, experienced, and wise woman, tempered and developed by the fires of life. She is an exceptional woman qualified to encourage and nurture, counsel, and advise, as well as support and mentor young women and girls, guiding them through the seasons of their lives.

CONTENTS

PREFACE

GRANDMOTHERS EDUCATING MINDS

As I began to draft this book, the essence of a grandmother filled my mind and heart, along with the many others like her whose love and nurturing spirit guided their families and a host of others around them.

It occurred to me that a grandmother's motto could be the same as the postman's creed:

> Through storm, or hail, or dark of night.

She is always there. She nurses the sick, helps the heavy-laden, and lifts the downtrodden. She shares her wisdom and timeless knowledge. But one attribute that makes her priceless is the thread that ties her together with all the other grandmothers throughout the ages, women of rich inner substance that enables them to display 'courage under fire.'

I remember wonderful things about my grandmother. Chapter two of this book tells her story and how she addressed many crises, the road she walked, the things she experienced, and the strength it took her to persevere through tough times.

She was only married once, but the marriage didn't last. She was left alone to raise four young girls on her own. She never remarried, believing that once a woman was married, even if the man left her, she was not to marry as long as he was still alive. She directed her strength toward raising her fatherless girls. She leaned on the Lord and passed Him forward from generation to generation as grandmothers and seasoned women do. They display wisdom, knowledge, and courage when facing challenges and tough times.

I have learned that the standard for addressing crises has not changed. History constantly and consistently repeats itself. Seasoned women, GEM's such as you, have a lot to contribute in light of the problems people face today.

My grandmother fulfilled her life by being a living example to younger women. She is one of the women that Apostle Paul speaks of in Titus 2:4, those who "teach the young women to be sober, to love their husbands, to love their children."

Many people claim that social or ethnic backgrounds are barriers that potentially inhibit one's capacity and potential to become the model of grace, but that is a sad and dreadful deception from the enemy of our souls; as you become partners with Christ, you will find your place among the women of Titus 2:4 Such women are enabled by the Spirit to avoid the web of carnal preoccupations with the opinions and attitudes of peers, family and even those in the church that do not look through eyes of grace. My grandmother understood that the views of others paled in comparison to life in the strength of the truths that God had entrusted to them as part of their belief systems. For the most part, how a person is spiritually or mentally equipped to handle a crisis plays a pivotal role in how they will respond to any crisis. In "My Tribute to My GEM," I mention that my grandmother did not request nor need external validation or preferential treatment, not even a pat on the back. She knew she had her treasure in heaven.

This book is designed to encourage you to seek and stand on the Word of God. It is written to inspire you to seek the guidance of the Holy Spirit, who will faithfully guide you into all truth. God's truth will reveal and connect the true meanings of life through the scriptures. It will enable you to help others, especially the young women of the twenty-first century.

Our young women must understand that a lot of what they do is because of the spiritual battle that took place between good and evil in Genesis 3. The Word of God is the only way we should address crises. If our young women don't understand why they think the way they do, their struggles will continue unabated.

The battle of the mind is a spiritual one. These young women will need the wisdom and guidance you provide to model the difference between right and wrong. In addition, you will teach them how the lack of understanding can leave them with conflicting and confusing thoughts.

God has an answer for every tragedy and crisis.

Apostle Paul wrote to the Corinthians, "In whom the god of this world hath blinded the minds of them which believe not, lest the light of the glorious gospel of Christ, who is an image of God, should shine unto them" - 2 Corinthians 4:4.

Young women do not know that the fall of Adam and Eve in the Garden of Eden transformed the soul of mankind into a battlefield for the war between God and Satan. God's ultimate plan to defeat Satan will happen. GEMs will teach young women that they can defeat Satan regardless of the battles threatening to overtake their personal lives by putting faith in God.

To paraphrase Ephesians 6:10-18, His subtle deception and lies are at the root of their problems. Our struggles and fight are not with one another but with the powers of darkness. But we have the power to overcome."

My GEM taught me to go to God for everything that concerns me, every burden, and He will answer my prayers through faith. The Bible clearly states, "He will deliver us from this present evil world, according to the will of God and our Father" - Galatians 1:4.

As you walk into your destiny as a GEM, you let every young woman that God places in your path know that He has addressed and fulfilled His plan for the crisis regarding the human sin nature. He never said it would be easy; He said to have faith in Him.

God understands our fallen state; he knew the battle was one we could not win without Him. Therefore, he gave His written Word to equip us for the battles and the blessings of life. He came to earth in the person of Jesus over 2,000 years ago. He gave His life as a sacrifice for sins to satisfy the justice of God so that God could forgive sins and make people righteous. He wants you to know and understand that His willingness to sacrifice His only Son proves His love for you.

He is well aware of how you think and what you will do before you do it. When no one else can help you, God is always there to help you overcome the crisis. He will never turn His back on you. John 3:16 says, "For God so loved the world that He gave His only begotten Son."

Why? Because "whosoever believeth on Him shall not perish but have everlasting life."

He loves all of us, and He does not want to lose anyone, not even our young women that are a little rough around the edges. He is the potter, and we are the clay. He took time out to mold us and make us. He wants us to pass the blessing forward to be the Titus 2:4 women we are designed and equipped to be. Our young women and girls are not spiritually equipped to fight every battle. This is another reason they need us. It is time to prepare the young women for the challenge so you may walk in your destiny.

A Special Thought:

THE ROLE OF THE SEASONED WOMAN

> To every thing there is a season, and a time to every purpose
> under the heaven: A time to be born, and a time to die; a
> time to plant, and a time to pluck up that which is planted;

— ECCLESIASTES 3:1-2

> The aged women, likewise, that they be in behavior as
> becometh holiness not false accusers, not given too much
> wine, teachers of good things;
> That they may teach the young women to be sober, to love
> their husbands, to love their children;
> To be discreet, chaste, keepers at home, good, obedient to their
> own husbands, that the word of God be not blasphemed

— TITUS 2:3-5

> A full age is the reward of piety

— JOB 5:26; GENESIS 15:15

We are the next generation's teachers. Let us all tell our story well so that we can finish strong. Author a book that will tell your history, fortunes, and pitfalls. Share wisdom keys that will spread down through the generations. I am still telling my story and the lessons I've learned. You've spurred me on to finish it.

NOT EQUIPPED FOR THE WAR

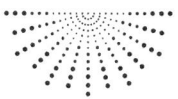

The ministry and the art of equipping our young women require wisdom, both for them and those who stand with them as mentors of grace.

Many of today's young women suffer from the crises they face daily. They make decisions based on how they feel at any given moment without thinking of the long-term implications and impacts. They lack understanding of how the battles of life work and the help that is there as the GEMs step in to guide them before the circumstances of their lives spiral out of control. In their spiritual immaturity and their inability to trust in God, they are often paralyzed by the fear of the unknown.

A seasoned woman and GEM has the wisdom to pick up the signs that indicate a crisis is ensuing. If she is familiar with the individual, she will be able to compare earlier behavior patterns with current ones. During face-to-face conversations, doors of understanding will begin to open simply as a mentor listens to the sound of a young lady's voice and especially her fear in her voice that signals helplessness.

There are, of course, many tell-tale signs and symptoms of someone who is in a state of crisis, including:

- uncontrollable crying
- displays of anxiety
- cutting classes
- food binges or not eating at all
- despair
- apprehension
- stomach aches and headaches
- sudden changes in appearance
- lashing out
- new friends leading them in the wrong direction
- feelings of panic or defeat.

Without proper guidance, a young woman may try anything and everything to solve her problem. Still, she will face over and over again the deep despair of failure. She will look for ways to escape from her situation. She may look to drugs, alcohol, sex, gang life, self-abuse such as cutting. She will, with few exceptions, try any means to escape, including the mindlessness of retreating into extreme levels of sleep. Each of these detours only drags them deeper into fear and hopelessness because they cannot manage their dilemmas alone. Those who do not yet have a relationship with God are not aware of the growth and guidance He provides to lead them through the valley of such darkness. Younger hearts struggling to free themselves desperately need the comfort and guidance of seasoned women to shine a new light into the dark, bleak valleys of their despair.

The message of Titus 2:4 encapsulates God's plan of action. Clearly, we have work to do.

Our high calling is to stand strong and make a difference in the lives of those God has lovingly placed in our lives. Everything we do, our plans and goals, and expectations should be centered on touching the lives of others with works of kindness. If God has brought us through the challenges and crises of life, we have a responsibility to extend that grace and comfort to others so that they can discover God's victory as well - 2 Corinthians 1:4. As we guide others to make sound decisions for their lives, they, in turn, will be able to touch others with the same touch of grace.

Sharing our stories of God's grace and mercy in our lives, how the Lord provided the opportunity to emerge from the valleys and traps in life shines the light of hope for their futures. As they see that we made it, they can begin to realize that there are real possibilities for them as well.

But sharing our stories needs more than our words. As followers of Jesus, we are to become vested in the lives of those God wants to touch through us. When we look at the story of Lazarus in John 11:35, we discover that people saw how much He was invested in Lazarus' life when they watched as "Jesus wept" over the death of His close friend. Jesus felt the pain of loss just as we feel the pain of loss.

To speak truth and grace into the lives of others must go beyond mere words of wisdom but must reveal to them how much we value them. Only then will they begin to realize that God loves them as well.

The next generation of young women are not prepared to face the struggles of life because they do not have the benefit of wiser, seasoned Christian women around them to help them steer their ways through the minefields of life ahead of them.

None of us will get through this life crisis-free. Obstacles will come into all our lives, maybe even send us on a detour or two, but we do not face them alone, nor are we to let others face those times in their lives on their own.

Whether our crises are big or small, when someone is there to respond with us, the impact and effect of those moments can noticeably change. What might have developed into something that could potentially destroy us becomes an occasion of grace as Godly women come alongside us and bring their strength and compassion to support us.

Spiritually seasoned women have become equipped by grace to tackle many different challenges. They have experienced what it means to be accountable to their family, friends, and strangers. In turn, they have built and cultivated those kinds of relationships with others whom they sense a responsibility to nurture. They become encouragers and nurturers in the lives of those who one day will be seasoned women as well.

In the following chapter, you will read the remarkable story of one of those seasoned women. She was my grandmother and a woman who passionately followed her calling to minister grace in the lives of others.

But my grandmother was no stranger to crises. She faced obstacles but did not walk in defeat. Struggles did not steal her love for God nor her awareness of His love for her. Battles did not leave her bitter but better able to move forward in her own life and reach out with great care and compassion to others, investing in the lives of others, especially the younger women around her, including her family. She is, of course, not the only GEM out there, but she is the one who changed my life. Her story gave birth to the vision for this book.

A TRIBUTE TO MY GRANDMOTHER

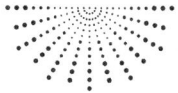

M s. Alberta M. Sadler was a diamond in the rough who became a GEM of beauty. I called her Mimi, and she was my grandmother. She was also a magnificent, seasoned woman.

You will not find her name in lights or on billboards. If you Google her name, you will not find some celebrated biographies or her face on the cover of Time Magazine. Nor will Forbes Magazine contain any pages detailing her net worth. But Alberta Marie Sadler was a GEM who was so extraordinary that the only book worthy of including her name is the Lamb's Book of Life.

My grandmother was a treasure. She was here for a moment in time, weaving a tapestry of life's lessons throughout the decades. Like a precious stone tossed into a crystal sea, her powerful legacy and priceless wisdom ripples from generation to generation in my family. Her legacy includes a wealth of love, matriarchal status, respect, and noteworthy accomplishments, all written indelibly in the hearts of those she loved and who loved her.

She exemplified a passion for God and family. She was utterly committed to following the examples of our Lord Jesus Christ. Her legacy also included serving joyfully in her church as a shining servant of grace. This role allowed her to leave a mark for Christ.

She never sought nor needed external validation or recognition. Some who knew her might have said she was unsung, overlooked, and unnoticed. They might even say that others took advantage of her. But she did not see it that way. She was a woman who exhibited great love, loyalty, and gratitude, but clearly without pretense

My grandmother was a strong advocate for education. Yet, she sacrificed her formal education so her children would not go without the things they needed. But she did not neglect her spiritual education. She read the Bible fervently and learned at the feet of Jesus through her prayer life. She was a mighty woman of prayer.

Born in the farmlands of Carrollton, Kentucky, my grandmother's journey took her to Indiana, where she became what later was called "a domestic engineer." However, she wore the label of "home maker" proudly until the opportunity came for her to take computer classes specializing in data entry. When that door opened, it allowed her to do more for her children with her income as a night-shift keypunch operator at a bank.

She single-handedly raised four children, burying one of her twin daughters at the tender age of five. And in time, she played a pivotal role in helping raise her grandchildren, which included me.

Through everything, she found the joy of the Lord. Mimi never lost sight of God's faithfulness to take her through whatever came her way. Although the "whatever's" of life are not always wonderful experiences but entrusted to God's care, they can build strong character. God allows us to encounter tests and trials to refine our awareness that He is our strength. That dependence on Him perfects us and enables us to edify His Kingdom. I will always be indebted to her for living her faith so vividly and sharing the invaluable lessons of her life with me.

One thing above all else that stood out in Mimi's life was her depth and irrepressible reverence for the Lord. Every Sunday, she found her way to her pew with genuine anticipation of the joy of worship and the Word. In addition, she attended Bible studies, auxiliary meetings, and a host of social events, all a part of her worship life.

My grandmother's faithfulness to God and her church became the foundation stones of my own spiritual life.

When my parents or grandmother went to church, so did I. But they did not attend the same church. They weren't even part of the same denomination. Mimi was Methodist; my parents were Baptists.

I guess you could say I was raised in a spiritually cross-cultural with different churches and different doctrinal emphasis. But I had no complaints. I loved going to church. I sang in the choir, loved the Bible stories, and made many friends. My mother told me I would quote scriptures, sing songs, and frequently say, "Lord give me strength," An expression I probably picked up from my grandmother.

Mimi was a tall, statuesque renaissance woman. She had a regal countenance and a beautiful smile. She was an impeccable dresser and had a fantastic wardrobe. She carried herself like a queen. Her perfumes were memorable and heavenly; after she would dress, out came the fragrance of the day and permeated her room with her scent.

Quite often, in one quick swoop, I would disappear into her room, where I enjoyed sampling her perfumes and playing in her closet. She had such beautiful clothes. I would stand there gazing at all the hat boxes or looking at the high-heeled shoes on the closet floor just before descending on the scarves and hats. My feet would clink and clank awkwardly across the wood floors in her high-heeled shoes. How could I deny myself the experience of reveling in the joy of playing grown-up?

Many times, she wasn't around for me to ask if I could put on some of her things, I am sure that she knew I was in her belongings, but she never said anything to me.

Getting ready for church was a big to-do on the level of an event in our home, one that always included a big breakfast. Then Mimi would continue preparing the Sunday meal, which she usually started on Saturday. She loved to cook. The aroma still fills my memories today. I enjoyed watching her bake. She would pull my chair up to the counter, and I would watch her make the most delectable pies and cakes. I could always count on her to put a little scoop of filling on a spoon for me to sample.

We would then get dressed for church. My Mimi would look so pretty, always smiling; she would put on one of her church hats with one hand while picking up her purse and gloves with the other hand. You see, in those days, a lady knew that an outfit was not complete until you had all the accessories in hand.

Mimi also made sure I had some of the loveliest dresses. Wearing my shiny black patent leather shoes, socks with ruffles, and with my small purse and gloves, I was all grown-up walking into the church holding Mimi's hand.

She made Sundays special. We could always expect company after Sunday service. Our home was warm, loving and full of laughter, so our place was regularly filled with company. They would sit around our dining room table and in the living room, and I reveled in hearing their stories and laughter. And Mimi sat with them beaming and laughing, her face filled with the warmth of her smile. Everyone loved Mimi, and Mimi obviously loved everybody.

Mimi displayed all the attributes highlighted by the Proverbs 31 woman. She was a provider and a woman who was known for her wisdom. Kindness flowed from her tongue. She blessed her children and family, along with a host of others; people rose up to call her "blessed." She was a woman whose reverence for the Lord caused others to think of her when they read the description of the virtuous woman.

Who can find a virtuous woman? For her price is far above rubies. The heart of her husband doth safely trust in her, so that he shall have no need of spoil. She will do him good and not evil all the days of her life. She seeketh wool, and flax, and worketh willingly with her hands.

She is like the merchants' ships; she bringeth her food from afar. She riseth also while it is yet night, and giveth meat to her household, and a portion to her maidens. She considereth a field, and buyeth it: with the fruit of her hands, she planteth a vineyard. She girdeth her loins with strength, and strengtheneth her arms. She perceiveth that her merchandise is good: her candle goeth not out by night. She layeth her hands to the spindle, and her hands hold the distaff. She stretcheth out her hand to the poor; yea, she reacheth forth her hands to the needy.

She is not afraid of the snow for her household: for all her household are clothed with scarlet. She maketh herself coverings of tapestry; her clothing is silk and purple. Her husband is known in the gates, when he sitteth among the elders of the land. She maketh fine linen, and selleth it; and delivereth girdles unto the merchant.

Strength and honour are her clothing; and she shall rejoice in time to come. She openeth her mouth with wisdom; and in her tongue is the law of kindness. She looketh well to the ways of her household, and eateth not the bread of idleness. Her children arise up, and call her blessed; her husband also, and he praiseth her. Many daughters have done virtuously, but thou excellest them all. Favour is deceitful, and beauty is vain: but a woman that feareth the Lord, she shall be praised.

Give her of the fruit of her hands; and let her own works praise her in the gates.

— PROVERBS 31:10-31

This proverb describes Mimi:

1. a woman of wisdom with the law of kindness in everything she said.
2. a brave, honest, strong person of integrity.
3. a lady of honor and strength
4. one blessed and revered by her family

Mimi's influence in my life, along with the examples set by my parents, accounts for much of what I am today. Of course, there were other influences in my family circle, but none like Mimi.

As I've explained, Mimi had a deep passion for God. She grew up in the small town of Carrollton, Kentucky, in the late 1920s. She was the only black person in her class, and her mother was only one generation removed from slavery. As a result, she instilled high moral standards in Mimi.

Mimi was a hardworking woman who was not always treated with the utmost respect, yet she knew who she was. Despite many doors being closed to her as she grew up, she stood firm in the face of adversity. As a black woman, she did not allow mistreatment because of her skin color to make her bitter. Instead, her love and vertical relationship with the Savior instilled the spirit to overcome obstacles.

Sadly, Mimi's husband found companionship in the arms of another and left her with four young daughters. Yet, the challenge of a failed marriage did not get in her way. As a divorcee and mother of four, she maintained a strong resolve to model strength for her children. She was not the kind of woman who looked for an easy way out, and she handled her responsibilities. Rather, she was a God-fearing woman, virtuous in all her ways whose focus on faith was evident.

Her daughters were Delores, the oldest; the twins, Fay and Kay; and the baby girl, Joan, my mother. Kay died from pneumonia at the age of five. When death knocked on the door, though her heart was broken,

Mimi picked herself up in the power of the Savior, and pressed through this painful loss, refused to walk in defeat.

She was a woman of a remarkable degree of dignity. To care for her three daughters, she did her best. Worked untiringly, doing domestic chores to make ends meet. She scrubbed floors on her hands and knees, washed and ironed clothes for other families, cared for their children as if they were her own, all to make sure her daughters would have a meal to eat. Yet, at the end of each of those long days, she returned to her own home overflowing with a nurturing spirit, passing out hugs and kisses. The words of Proverbs 31:25 that speak of "strength and honor are her clothing" describe Mimi perfectly. Those virtues beamed from and flowed unhindered into the lives of others, but especially those in her family. She set the bar high for us to follow.

The three sisters took care of each other while their mother worked. In those days, the oldest girl helped with the younger siblings. The elder daughters took on responsibilities in the home until they were financially able to move out on their own, left for college, or were married.

Mimi thrived under some of the most challenging circumstances. She raised three wonderful daughters, and her sacrifices allowed them to become incredible women of substance and character. My late aunt Delores was an accountant with a career that spanned more than thirty-five years. My late aunt Fay was a paralegal for more than three decades. My mother has been a nurse for thirty-six years and still holds a current LPN license. Mimi never let the absence of a husband or a father for her children hinder her commitment to nor extinguish her hopes and dreams for her daughter's lives.

Mimi was a force of grace that flowed over and through all our lives.

3
CHANGING TIMES

An abrupt change interrupted life as I had known it during my childhood.

My parents uprooted us from life in the city and relocated to a place called Plainfield, Indiana. Not only did we have to leave Mimi, which was devastating enough by itself, but we were plopped down in the open and what felt like the emptiness of country life. I felt like Dorothy - being blown into the strange life of Oz. The change was a real jolt. I was not a happy camper. When my parents would take me to visit my grandmother, the separation after each visit was painful. I would cry from the moment I would cry from the moment I left her home until I fell asleep in the car returning to Plainfield. It was a culture shock attending a new school in Plainfield away from my familiar surroundings . Until I showed up, it was not integrated. I was the only African American student in the entire East Grade school. I think I was the only African American little girl in my neighborhood for miles around.

Later in life, I came to understand why the move was necessary. My father found a better-paying job. It was essential to move because he needed the job to take better care of his family. It was hard for black men to find good-paying jobs in those days.

After three years of going back and forth visiting my grandmother, my mother delivered some important news. My mother's nursing career was taking off. She was hired at a hospital, and my father chose to commute between the two cities for the next thirty years when he retired. But, for me, the only thing the news meant was that we were moving back to be with Mimi. I was returning to the familiar, to the rest of my family and friends. I was beyond excited. And it meant that I would return to my old school. Integration had come to the area, and the school system was busing children in and out of the district. I did not realize, of course, that in those few short years, my whole neighborhood had changed drastically from what I remembered.

It was hard readjusting to city culture, fitting into the different surroundings, and unfamiliar faces. The new kids in school were not from my neighborhood. I was constantly teased about the way I dressed, my skin color, and even derided because I talked "proper," not the slang and trendy expressions that had infiltrated the place that had once been filled with the comfort of the familiar.

I often cried about the rejection I felt from the other children. Having never experienced this type of treatment, I wished I could have gone back to the country with my other friends. Fear gripped my heart, and the early stages of low self-esteem began to develop. But with time the guidance of my grandmother, first and foremost, I toughened up, adapted to my new surroundings. Her wisdom helped me deal with the meanness of other children. Because of her own experiences, Mimi taught me how to maintain my focus despite my surroundings. She taught me not to allow negative opinions of others to take root in my life and not to let others kill my dreams.

My teachers also took an interest in me, stepping in to help me adjust and stand up for myself. I learned to concentrate and focus on my schoolwork. I discovered and developed my interests. As I reflect upon that time, I appreciate the security and support that I had. Mimi cared, not demanding anything in return. My teachers were wonderful as well. They took an interest in me, mentoring and guiding me as well. As the African proverb says, "It takes a village to raise a child."

As my mother and I discussed the writing of this book, we acknowledged that a significant part of our family's history, including this readjustment, was deeply interlocked with the story and influences of my grandmother. This is one of the things that motivated me to write this account of her life.

4

THE LONG GOODBYE

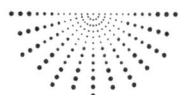

As time went by, my grandmother began to exhibit signs of dementia. Dementia is a debilitating disease that causes the degeneration or loss of nerve cells in the brain, just like Parkinson's and Huntington's disease. It is also known as the "long goodbye" since the person experiences accelerated memory loss and loses the ability to communicate.

In the end, dementia took Mimi's ability to give hugs, smile, or share a meal. Her voice was silenced both by those who loved her and those she had so deeply loved. The holiday celebrations, barbecues, weddings, family reunions, her delicious recipes, and most of all, her Godly advice were all locked up somewhere within the recesses of her mind. That is when I realized that her stories were shared. The essence of who she was would go silent. While her influence will live on in those of us who had caught her mantel, the record of her life of grace and compassion could find a fresh voice once again.

Then came the day the inevitable happened. Mimi, my GEM, went home to be with the Lord at the age of ninety-two. As she was leaving the restraints of this world, we all looked at each other in silence, facing together the reality that she was leaving us.

No one in our family can ever remember her uttering a single complaint. If she did complain, she took it to Jesus. For it was in Him that she found her strength and the grace to continue. Due to her adoration and love for Christ, we have the rich heritage to love and serve others. She left us with faith, hope, and a strong tenacity for life with a spirit of endurance that truly defies description.

She passed the love of God to us so that we, in turn, might pass His love to the next generation and then the next after that. Thus, her place as my GEM was physically fulfilled but with a heritage of spiritual echoes that will ripple across the waters of my life and into the lives of others.

Mimi gave a piece of herself for each of us to carry and pass on to those around us. She left us light, her light that was shown with His light. She would say these simple words: "Love God, and love people." She was a "seasoned woman." She was a remarkable GEM.

As I stood before her at that moment, the memories of what she had deposited into my life played across my mind like a kaleidoscope of grace and truth. Knowing this, I will always try to live a life that honors her and her teachings.

Mimi was a gift from God. I still have feelings of profound loss that arise from time to time, especially when I say something to my children or grandchildren that remind me of her. The wealth of Godly wisdom she left has impacted my life significantly. My love for her and the cherished memories will always live in my heart.

Today, it blesses me to see my children and grandchildren all walking in a passionate personal relationship with the Lord shining into the lives of others. Nothing can be more gratifying than to know that your family knows Christ as Lord and Savior.

My grandmother's challenges are not unlike some of the challenges young women face today. In remembering her triumphs, it is my hope and purpose that her commitment to a life of faith and a passion for others will become the legacy of this book.

5

GEMS THROUGH THE AGES

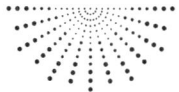

Grandmothers Educating Minds and its focus on the seasoned woman embodies the essence of family legacies. These women sustain, organize, and direct families they rightfully can be proud of. They and their families are who they are regardless of the origin of their heritage. They fully understand that the most important thing in life is the family, specifically those who discovered the power and light of faith.

One's family history also enables the younger generation to feel the honor and responsibility of being part of something more important than themselves, regardless of ethnicity or family origin, heritage, and values cultivated. Not every aspect of one's ancestry is pristine. The annals of history are full of those who came before that cultivated legacies of failed, even destructive influences.

The scriptures are full of good and not-so-good examples of leaders. From Jochebed, the mother of Moses, to the evil Athaliah, grandmother of young King Joash who for the most of his life reigned as a good king despite his grandmother; to Mary, the mother of our Savior, the 'hand that rocked the cradle,' who has been a significant influence throughout the ages. The Old Testament has far more bad examples than good ones, but from each comes important lessons. History, as a whole, is the same. For example, the history of slavery was not, and is not, the sum total of the African American experience. While African American families were torn asunder by many factors, out of those times, an unseen benefit appeared in the form of seasoned women who were the backbone of their families. Their presence became the guiding lights in a culture of struggle and oppression.

Out of that period came some powerful figures such as the intellectual Mary McLeod Bethune-Cookman, who went from teaching in schoolhouses that were often little more than shanties, where they advocated for freedom, to being received as dignitaries at the White House. Harriet Tubman was deemed the "Black Moses" for her relentless fight against slavery and racism. Her extraordinary contribution paved the way for the Underground Railroad. She was a pivotal figure that led to thousands finding freedom in America.

Such are the stories of our grandmothers, the seasoned women, who became the glue that held families together and built legacies that have impacted generations.

These remarkable and noteworthy women never sought to be significant figures of history, yet that is quite rightly what they became. Each did what they had to do to survive with a single purpose of lovingly protecting their families and others who shared their lives. So often, GEMs are unaware of how vital they are in changing the lives of others. Most were unsung heroes with no significant evidence of riches nor educational credentials. Yet, their spiritual commitment and passion redefined the personal asset of selflessness focused on lifting others from their despair as one of the most powerful factors that redefined a community and even a nation.

That is the calling of the seasoned woman of today. Her God-ordained role is to be a tool in God's hand to spread the knowledge and wisdom of grace and hope. These are the ones who leave legacies, promote pride and confidence in individuals, and they do it all with remarkable humility.

Grandmothers are the guiding scepters of strength. They are the protectors. Their honest words touch our hearts. Even when those honest words are not what we want to hear, the answers they have for us are full of wisdom. We leave their presence with a sense of peace, understanding, and truth. We can share our dreams, heartbreaks, and struggles with the GEM in our lives with an assurance that her prayers will touch the heart of God, and His wisdom, blessing, direction, and interventions will rain down and set us free.

Though we may have often been told to hush up, listen well, or "stay in a child's place," the loving heart of such a grandmother invites us to come close and open our hearts to hers. She is ready to listen, understand, and have the passion for sharing the wisdom of the ages with us.

If we are willing to listen with respect and genuine attentiveness, our history and family values come alive through the caring counsel of these women. We learn that although grandpa, grandmother, and our older family members may not have had formal education or were offered many opportunities, they used their God-given gifts and knowledge, along with their various crafts, skills, and trades, to develop profitable careers which they were able to pass down. Their hard work also affords us, as their children, the opportunities for advancements in careers they were never able to realize.

We learn that strong family dynasties have a common denominator; loving God and loving to serve others. These two truths can turn an attitude from merely surviving to being successful, prosperous, and thriving. Seasoned women and grandmothers pass these truths on to future generations and will continue to do so with the help of God.

Their examples demonstrate that strength and success in life come through the joy and privilege of living for Christ. That kind of strength is waiting to be awakened in the minds and hearts of young women today. They are waiting for guidance from today's seasoned women and grandmothers.

As seasoned older women, we can tap into what lies deep within these young women. These young souls must be cultivated by the seasoned women God has placed in their lives whose care and compassion can stimulate the dreams and hopes of greatness that lie within each one of them. The responsibility is ours.

6
RELEVANCE

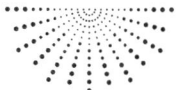

Unfortunately, the importance of the seasoned woman and grandmother is being forgotten, unappreciated, and lost. Today many with years of experience and understanding are being disregarded. Some find themselves being placed into assisted-living facilities only for the sake of convenience. Their wealth of information and insight is no longer appreciated. Their beauty is being ignored, and they aren't receiving the reverence that is due to them.

The day may come when residential or nursing home care may be a necessary place for our loved ones. But, unfortunately, too often, they are placed there and forgotten. Too many rarely receive visits or are taken to relatives' homes for a decent meal or family time. They are viewed as too slow, unable to keep up, unimportant, or too old or confused to understand or appreciate what is going on these days.

These are the women who filled us with infinite wisdom and knowledge. We can learn so much from them. From their experiences and wisdom, we are enabled to live productive and meaningful lives. The insight and values stored within them can still equip future generations to succeed and live meaningful lives. They invested their hearts in ours; it is time for us to invest our hearts in them

It is sobering that this priceless reservoir can be so easily lost. Such wealth is fragile.

In our culture of individualism, our instinct is focused on ourselves. Our ego-centric mantras produced chants in one form or another that declared, "You take care of yours, and I will take care of mine." As a result, the value of community fades into the background of our lives. "It takes a village" is relegated to a wish list or one of our lofty ideals. It is time to remember, appreciate, embrace, and value the voices of those who in wisdom call us to set aside our selfishness and pick up the touch of faith and compassion that with a proper sense of humility lets us "esteem other(s) better than (our)selves" - Philippians 2:3. The GEMs who spoke those truths to us also modeled them for us, and both their words and lives have made us who we are. As we allow their lives of compassion to embed themselves deep within us, we become people with a deep sense of accountability.

It is also time for us to shake off any measure of lethargy and wrap our minds around the responsibility that falls increasingly on our shoulders. May the grand ideas and purposes that lie dormant in our lives come alive and give birth to the noble goal of becoming Godly change agents in the hearts and minds of those young women who are searching for someone to come alongside them. The dreams and hopes that have become a part of our lives were passed on to us by our GEMs. As we grow older, the voices of our GEMs inspire us to amass our own storehouses of wisdom from our seasons of trial, error, challenge, and triumph. And it is our biblical and moral obligation to pour ourselves into those young women who will come after us.

I must say again that the purpose of this book is to be a voice that gives birth within you the determination and the confidence to go forward and embrace your calling to become a seasoned woman, and a true GEM for other young women.

REFLECTION

No matter how challenging life may be at times, precious memories will emerge for those willing to look for them. The "Reflection" pages are provided so you can reflect on your days and begin to record those gems of your own. Gather your thoughts here so that later in your life, you can deposit them into the lives of others. The person who had the most significant influence in my life during my childhood was:

_____
_____
_____
_____
_____

What role did they play? How did they influence your life?

_____
_____
_____
_____
_____

What was the greatest piece of advice, or words of wisdom, ever given to you?

_____
_____
_____
_____
_____

How have you integrated those words into your everyday life thus far?

_____

_____

_____

_____

_____

THE IMPORTANCE OF BEING RELEVANT

Do you know what relevance means? It is from the noun relevant, which means "pertinent." You are pertinent. You matter.

Is there a seasoned woman or grandmother who is part of your life with whom you've lost contact? Is there someone who has come to mind in reading this book that has been a tremendous influence in the lives of others? Perhaps they've been forgotten by their family or friends. How would you get in touch with them, and what would you do once you make that contact?

Put down your thoughts and your plan of contact.

_____
_____
_____
_____
_____
_____
_____
_____
_____
_____
_____
_____
_____
_____
_____
_____
_____
_____
_____
_____
_____
_____

7

THE PURPOSE OF THE SEASONED WOMAN

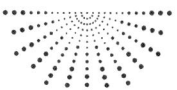

The Lord has established a way of life for all of us.

As grandmothers and seasoned women, we are to find joy and peace in God's plan for our daily lives. Passing the torch is part of life's design. Deciding to center our lives in Christ is a choice to pass on significance and value to our children.

In Ecclesiastes 3, we are told that everything has a time and season. The seasons of our lives will vary, but we will cross paths with a variety of people in all of them. Throughout our lifetimes, we are blessed with great opportunities, an abundance of possessions, and a wealth of discoveries – all of which can add value to our lives. Still, the only part of our lives that will last us is what we do for Christ with all the things He has allowed us to have.

The Bible says, in Luke 6:38, "Give, and it shall be given unto you." I speak from experience when I say that as I let go of what is in my hand, God lets go of what is in His hand. He receives from me my all, but His "all" is greater than mine. All authority in heaven and earth rests in God. In response to our meager gifts, God opens the windows of Heaven and pours out measures of blessings that exceed our requests or even our imaginations. And one of those immeasurable blessings is the privilege of passing on to others the torch of grace and compassion that is part of God's design for our lives.

God has placed each of us here for this specific time, season and purpose. The Lord is diligently at work, faithfully unfolding an earthly plan in our lives. Although the parable of the ten talents speaks of money, it speaks directly to God's His purpose for us to invest what we have received from His hand so that those coming behind us will reap grace and peace. "Paying it forward" is not a new idea. God has built within us an instinct to do just that.

> And unto one he gave five talents, to another two, and to another one; to every man according to his several abilities; and straightway took his journey. Then he that had received the five talents went and traded with the same, and made them another other five talents. And likewise, he that had received two, he also gained other two. But he that had received one went and digged in the earth, and hid his lord's money.
> After a long time, the lord of those servants cometh, and reckoneth with them. And so he that had received five talents came and brought other five talents, saying, Lord, thou deliveredst unto me five talents: behold, I have gained beside them five talents more. His lord said unto him, Well done, thou good and faithful servant: thou hast been faithful over a few things, I will make thee ruler over many things: enter thou into the joy of thy lord. He also that had received two talents came and said, Lord, thou deliveredst unto me two talents: behold, I have gained two other talents beside them.
> His lord said unto him, Well done, good and faithful servant; thou hast been faithful over a few things, I will make thee ruler over many things: enter thou into the joy of thy lord.
> Then he which had received the one talent came and said,

Lord, I knew thee that thou art an hard man, reaping where
thou hast not sown, and gathering where thou hast not
sowed: and I was afraid, and went and hid thy talent in the
earth: lo, there thou hast that is thine.

His lord answered and said unto him, Thou wicked and
slothful servant, thou knewest that I reap where I sowed
not, and gather where I have not sowed: Thou oughtest
therefore to have put my money to the exchangers, and then
at my coming I should have received mine own with usury.

Take therefore the talent from him, and give it unto him which
hath ten talents

— MATTHEW 25:15-28

This parable has a powerful message. We are to use everything the
Lord gives us: wisdom, employment, possession, and opportunities
for God's glory. We are to be productive stewards. We are not to
squander the gifts He has afforded us.

I once heard Dr. Myles Monroe say, "The richest land in the world is
the graveyard because there lies all the dreams and visions of those
who didn't act on God's plan."

Someone somewhere along our paths has a dream, but they need us to
sow into their lives to make that dream come true. Read what the
Apostle Paul states:

Be not deceived; God is not mocked; for whatsoever a man
soweth, that shall he also reap. For he that soweth to his
flesh shall of the flesh reap corruption; but he that soweth
to the Spirit shall of the spirit reap of life everlasting. And
let us not be weary in well doing: for in due season we shall
reap, if we faint not

— GALATIANS 5:7-8

We are so full of blessings. It is time to make our deposit into the young lives around us and not be like the man with the one talent, holding on to it for fear of losing it. If we share what we have, we can expect the blessings of the Lord to rain upon us. We don't want God to step in and take what He entrusted to us and give it away to another whose faithfulness is greater than ours.

PURPOSE

How would you answer someone if they were to ask, "Do you know what your purpose in life is?" The truth is that you may or may not know your purpose at this point. Perhaps you may have a fairly good idea, but you still need some clarity.

But here is a point to ponder. If you know that you will help others, then you may know more about God's plan for you than you may think. The specific appointments or steps that lay ahead in your journey will be made plain to you in God's own time, which by the way, will always be the perfect time.

REFLECTION

My favorite scripture is:

_____
_____
_____
_____
_____

I believe my purpose in life to be:

_____
_____
_____
_____
_____

Some of the challenges I am facing reaching the goal include:

_____
_____
_____
_____
_____

I plan to overcome them by:

_____
_____
_____
_____
_____

At this point in your life, what are you able to share with someone seeking wisdom and advice from you in a particular area or in general? For example, if a young person were to sit and talk with you and make the following statement, "I don't know what my purpose in life is," how do you think you would respond? What are you ready to pass on?

_____
_____
_____
_____
_____
_____
_____
_____
_____
_____
_____
_____
_____
_____
_____
_____
_____
_____
_____
_____
_____
_____
_____
_____
_____
_____

8

THE SEASONED WOMAN WHO WOULD BECOME A MENTOR: THE CRITERIA FOR A GEM

S easoned women genuinely care for people and are authentic in their desire to make a difference in the next generation of friends, family, strangers, and especially young women.

A seasoned woman is strong enough not to break under pressure, wise enough to know when to speak up, and prudent enough to know when to remain silent. The gift of discernment and judgment will help her guide those with whom she comes in contact, enlightening them with wisdom and counsel regarding the kinds of steps they need to take to uncover what God has designed for their best interests.

The seasoned woman must have a genuine desire to truly get to know someone and often love them despite themselves. She must be resilient enough to see a task or assignment through, investing enough of herself in the lives of others to be effective. She may have to try different approaches under God's guidance to reach a young woman because no two people are alike, but she persists because she is passionate.

To be a GEM, as you have probably already realized, a seasoned woman doesn't necessarily have to be a grandmother. I've frequently equated a GEM as a grandmother. But, of course, she doesn't have to be a biological grandmother. She may be a woman who carries the mantle of a grandmother.

Elisha was a prophet who shadowed his mentor, Elijah. When Elijah was caught up in the chariot of God, he caught the mantle of his mentor. Thus, the spirit of Elijah was passed on to his protégé Elisha.

The mantle or spirit of grace and compassion of the GEMs that molded our lives can fall on us, anointing us for our calling to be the GEM in someone else's life.

With this inherent blessing, GEMs are examples of mentoring models to their loved ones, co-workers, and friends throughout their communities. These women are lampposts whose purpose is to come alongside others and guide them through dark times.

A GEM is the embodiment of the unconditional love God imparts. She is acting at the prompting of God's Spirit. In the Greek language of the New Testament, the Spirit of God is often referred to as the Paraclete, which means "one who comes alongside." The heart of a GEM reflects the presence and prompting of the Paraclete, who is at work through her as she comes alongside others who need comfort and guidance.

She becomes that one who can show us a better way of life as she shares the wisdom she has gained throughout her achievements and mistakes. While such a seasoned woman is never perfect, she is still the instrument of grace, charged with the sacred privilege of touching others with the grace and comfort that God has extended in their lives 2 Corinthians 1:4-5.

This calling raises the inevitable question, "Will I rise to be such a role model?" Reaching this high calling requires a certain measure of self-evaluation in light of Titus 2: 3-5:

> The aged women, likewise, that they be in behavior as
>   becometh holiness, not false accusers, not given to much
>   wine, teachers of good things;
> That they may teach the young women to be sober, to love
>   their husbands, to love their children,
> To be discreet, chaste, keepers at home, good, obedient to their
>   own husbands, that the word of God be not blasphemed

It is reasonable to ask, "Will I be a woman of such spiritual substance? Am I willing to become the selfless person who will come alongside younger women and speak truth and grace into them even when they are not always willing to listen?

This charge we carry has the obligation that shapes everything we do to invest in the lives of those who come behind us.

REFLECTION: THE RECIPE OF ME

What are the ingredients that season your life and make you who you are? What are you made of?

This chapter discussed some of the attributes of a seasoned woman. Look at the list below. On a scale of 1-10, ten being the highest and one being the lowest, how do you see yourself, and why? Feel free to reflect on each and note your thoughts about improving in those areas.

Joyful

_____

_____

Open

_____

_____

Mature

_____

_____

Endurance

_____

_____

Encourager

_____
_____

Love People

_____
_____

If you could describe yourself as a spice or seasoning, which one would you be and why?

_____
_____
_____
_____
_____

Consider This

In the world we live in, the most expensive objects increase in value as they age. Seasoned women do too. Through the variety of life's experiences, the knowledge they amass is priceless.

As you continue your sojourn through life, hopefully with the words in this book to guide you, think about the following:

Do you have the zest for life expressed in the joy of sharing God's goodness with others? Can you display the maturity needed to keep cool in a crisis? Are you willing to share your experiences: the good, the bad, and the ugly? Can you display an undeniable strength and toughness when faced with a challenging situation?

Can you stand with someone during a crisis, going through it with them for a season or longer? Are you tempered enough to weather any storm? Are you ready to guide by example, impart your wisdom, and become a blessing to women who are in need?

I pray that as you continue to read this book and listen to the voice of the Spirit who comes alongside you, you will more fully realize the woman of substance you are becoming and indeed already are.

9

TONI'S SOAP BOX

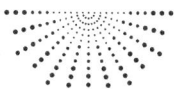

A WORD ABOUT SPIRITUAL ABORTION AND SPIRITUAL RESPONSIBILITY

Now that you've had time to think, reflect, and consider the characteristics and qualities you possess, it's time to delve into the more profound understanding of the calling in the heart of the seasoned woman.

This life of loving and mentoring will not always be sunshine or roses. No life is a flowery bed of ease. There will be tears. There will be pain. And prayerfully, in the end, there will be joy.

But first things first.

It is time to deal with certain realities that stare us in the face daily. We could, of course, use the common expression, "the elephant in the room," but that is hardly adequate. The reality I am referring to is more like a house on fire with society standing by watching it burn, like a bad B-movie.

Are you not sick and tired yet of how the news media exploits images of our children being arrested, missing, abused, or dead, often from the violence of our neighborhoods? When are we, seasoned Christian women, going to stop being comfortable watching our younger women and girls become the latest victims of moral decay? What is happening to them is nothing short of "spiritual abortion."

Every day I ask myself that question, and I know I can't be the only one that feels this way.

And it has become an even more nagging issue for me since I read an article written by Dr. Roger Barrier. He holds multiple degrees from Baylor University, Southwestern Baptist Theological Seminary, and Golden Gate Seminary in Greek language studies, religion, theology, and pastoral care. Dr. Barrier has coined the expression "spiritual abortion" to describe people who accept Jesus into their hearts at an early age, then never really do anything involving Him with their lives." These are the "still-born" saints that never experience a relationship with Christ that makes a difference in their lives, never act in faith, and consequently, never have influence in the lives of others.

Either they never truly heard the gospel and had a moment in which they had an emotional reaction. Still, nothing more, or they heard it but never really understood it and never fully received it, or they bailed out when the going got tough. They had not had a chance to mature enough to withstand the battle they faced. Whatever the case may be, they are so caught up in, even addicted to the things of this world, that the weeds of this life choked out the things of Christ.

Spiritual abortion happens when at any point, we fail to act at the prompting of the Spirit to grow in grace and knowledge of Christ and simply do not have the fortitude to resist the lures of the enemy. We fail because we lose our sense of spiritual purpose. Believers who keep their eyes on Christ, mature in their faith, discover a resolve to remain faithful to the end. True Believers know that there is nothing better than God and living the life He intended for them to live. Those who see life through our Lord's eyes and find their purpose in God do not abort their birth rights.

Dr, Barrier will never know the experience of a physical abortion. Yet, through the eyes of the Spirit, he has captured this profound spiritual image. His insight has provided us with a new expression that should have a powerful impact on our understanding. If we don't want the next generation to fall into the enemy's hands, we need to learn to call this travesty for what it is, a spiritual abortion. Not only do our words need to change, but our ways need to as well. The enemy is ready and willing to capture any "child" left to their own devices, left to die from neglect.

Just as physical abortion is a form of rejection, so spiritual abortion is equally so. The culture of rejection evident in this concept breeds other forms of rejection just as it does physically. Out of rejection, a profound and calloused insensitivity is birthed, which in turn produces other forms of other darkness that thrive and renders us blind as long as no one dares to shine the Light of Truth into the situation.

I wrote a poem that follows provides a powerful description of spiritual abortion.

THE VOICE OF SPIRITUAL ABORTION

God formed me and designed a plan for me before the
    foundations of the world,
I'm meant to be here, be heard, be relished, have a voice,
Am I worthy of you, don't steal your voice from me,
It's not my fault that you can't face your shames,
Don't make me suffer.

I'm a spiritual being, living in a body,
I need to learn about pure beauty, about my significance; I
    need you,
Don't steal your voice from me.
Without you, my world crumbles and falls apart,
The weight of my burdens follows me; I can't escape

I look around for a voice to speak wisdom,
You have hidden it from me,
I want to hear your voice of direction, your laughter, and
    insight; I have scars, wounds, and unspoken feelings.
Who should I trust, who shall I turn to?

The world is moving so fast; it doesn't know my voice, my gifts,
    my talents,
It is not God's plan for no one to want me,
It is selfish that you won't talk to me; this is unfair,
God trusted you with His plan; don't let my life be taken,

I would have respected you for trying,
I would have looked back one day and said, God had a plan for
    my life. I desperately need you, don't you miss my absence,
    and don't you wonder where I am,
Am I lovable? Am I worth your time?

Don't steal your voice from me,
Don't spiritually abort me; I will listen even if you think that I
    don't,
Don't spiritually abort me; I am a part of a bigger picture,
Don't spiritually abort me; I will make mistakes,

The thought of you turning your back on me hurts,
It sends me into a panic, a dark place, where I feel alone,
My voice becomes one of the negative actions,
Don't spiritually abort me, don't throw me away,
I don't understand, life, I'm silently screaming, "I am here, in
    need of you,"

I wonder if my life ends, did I do all God created me to be, or
    was I aborted,
Don't steal your voice from me,
Shhh, can you hear that Silence? It is not always golden,
Your silence is my spiritual abortion
Please, don't steal your voice from me.

— AUTHOR TONI KLECKLEY

REFLECTION

Perhaps this chapter and this poem bring to light an experience of your own. Maybe you walked through a valley of spiritual abortion in your own life, a time when you struggled, but no one was there to hear your pain.

Or perhaps you faced such a time when a disappointment, death of a dream, or devastating event, and because someone chose to steal their voice from you, the Savior was there to carry you through.

Perhaps what you have read has caused you to wonder how you will help those who may come to you or those in the midst of their crossroads.

Some have declared that we have turned our backs on our young women. Is this true? Have we adopted the world's mindset and direction by labeling these young women as unsalvageable?

Fortunately, I was not aborted. Instead, the voice of a seasoned woman spoke into my life and guided me through some of the tough times. And fortunately, you were not aborted. A voice sustained you and loved you.

Now, it is our turn to stand alongside those young women who lack maturity, are fragile, and are easily broken. We need to embrace them and be the voices that comfort and encourage them in their battles.

Based on the Spiritual Abortion poem and your life experience thus far, could you say this is something you've experienced? If so, how? Please take the time to write down your thoughts.

_____
_____
_____
_____
_____

How did it speak to you from the viewpoint of becoming a mentor to a person seeking your guidance? Do some or all the feelings reflected in this poem relate to you?

_____
_____
_____
_____
_____

Along with your counsel and encouragement, what scripture(s) could, or would you share with those for whom your voice rings with hope?

_____
_____
_____
_____
_____

10

LIVING IN A MATERIAL WORLD

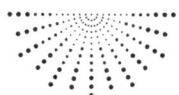

The media and the world system constantly bombard us with their doleful pronouncement of doom and gloom bolstered by their incessantly negative statistics regarding the young women in today's environment. But are we ready to settle for such dark projections painting their future as bleak and their lifespans as destined for tragedy and disappointment?

This is an urgent plea to reject the conclusions that our young women are irretrievably "at-risk," with their only possibility of being rescued coming at the deceptive smiles and devices of the same society that has created such a mess. But, unfortunately, the assessments from government programs and social awareness voices lack any real and substantive knowledge of our young women's lives other than those devised from the twisted social theories of academia and their darkened reasoning they blindly declare is enlightenment.

Let's be clear. Our young women are not statistics. They are people. We cannot allow negative generalizations to define them. We can either be a part of the problem or the solution.

Too often, we tend to sit back in our self-deceived comfort, passing judgment. We listen to their raucous music, staring with disapproval at all the piercings and tattoos, and react as if these are proof positive of flaws in their character. But the Titus 2:4 woman sees with different eyes and realizes that each of the younger set is not beyond nurturing. They look with grace and become aware of the potential each holds with the love and care of a GEM.

If we don't want them to fall, fail, and spiral out of control, we must change our attitudes and take action. We need to watch the words we use. We need to extend helping hands. To do otherwise is to willfully send these young women into the arms of illicit relationships, drugs, depression, false acceptance, deceit, and destructive lifestyles that are waiting to entrap them otherwise with embraces that eventually squeeze the life out of them

Within the Body of Christ, young women are to feel accepted. If they feel the sting of rejection from the GEMs or the seasoned women in the church, they will most likely leave the church, maybe never to return. The rejection these young women experience from certain church members can irreparably damage their perception of Christ.

This is how the many young women with whom I have spoken feel about the Church. When just one of them decides to walk away from the Church, we have become complicit in our spiritual abortion.

Yet, all of us have been on the Potter's wheel. None of us are perfect, and some of us have probably been on the wheel more than once. I know I have. How do we so callously deny grace to others when we have been privileged to be touched by grace in the middle of our own muddled days.

One of the current social issues we, as a church, cannot ignore is the pro-life vs. the pro-choice debate. Yet, I cannot help but pose the question in this context:is the Church pro-life or pro-choice?

Do we pick and choose which young women are worth saving and which are not? Are we miscarrying, aborting, and abandoning our spiritual lineage? Are we leaving them in the hands of the enemy to twist their minds and lead them to seek relationships that deceptively entice them with promises of security but only enslave them as objects of lust and abuse?

To those of us who are or want to be GEMs, let me remind you that we are all children of God seeking in this life to follow our Creator's plan. Christ loves us, died on the cross, and shed His blood for us as proof of how much He values us and how much we need to realize that He loves them just as deeply.

Luke 15:4-7 Jesus' parable of the lost sheep clearly states that we are to rejoice when even one soul is recovered.

> What man of you, having a hundred sheep, if he lose one of them, doth not leave the ninety and nine in the wilderness, and go after that which is lost until he find it? And when he hath found it, he layeth it on his shoulders, rejoicing. And when he cometh home, he calleth together his friends and neighbours, saying unto them, Rejoice with me; for I have found my sheep which was lost. I say unto you, that likewise joy shall be in heaven over one sinner that repenteth, more than over ninety and nine just persons, which need no repentance.

Count on it. There's more joy in heaven over one sinner's rescued life than over ninety-nine good people with no need of being saved. Such are our young women.

When one young woman is hurting, we all should hurt. Her pain should be our pain. Satan knows no boundaries. He will attempt to steal, kill, and destroy her by any means necessary. Trickery, cunning deception, and manipulation are his tools. He knows how to exploit those who are weak and unequipped with the Word of God. He preys on those who have not discovered the power to overcome spiritual battles through prayer.

One of the great tragedies in the Church is the inability of its members to feel the grief in God's own heart when young women are lost or hurt.

Our task is to equip these women to fight and survive the battles that await them in life. They are running to and fro, seeking to fulfill the desires of the flesh, without understanding that the void they are trying to fill is meant to be filled by God. He longs to supply their needs and give them the desires of their heart. When they learn to seek out His kingdom first, He will provide them with life and even life more than in abundant measure.

Without the Holy Spirit guiding their lives, young women are running smack dead into the traps of Satan. They are cohabiting or 'shacking up' with men whose only intent is to abuse and damage their tender young hearts. The purest feelings of love and trust are turned into scars of rejection, low self-esteem, and a deeply damaged self-worth.

What a contrast to God's plan for them! These are the young women who will grow up to make decisions that will affect future generations. It is our responsibility to guide them and model our faith before them.

Jesus, Himself, is our model for this kind of living. As He walked the dusty roads of Galilee, He was filled with compassion. He once looked over Jerusalem and grieved that His people were wandering around unprotected, like little chickens who would not run for shelter to their mothers. He would never have conceived that a single person in that great city was not worthy of the sacrifice He was prepared to make for them.

His life was a model of righteousness, yet Jesus lived by the example of the Father. Jesus clearly said that He only did what He could see the Father doing. As Jesus healed the sick, restored the broken-hearted, extended compassion, and even spoke words of rebuke, Jesus mentored those in His charge. Jesus was reflecting the image of the Father.

Jesus did not focus on how they looked on the outside. Those who had material means were invited to no longer trust in their possession but in Him. To the poor and needy, Jesus offered to supply them with what they needed. If they would quit chasing after earthly wealth, they could inherit life under the care of His Kingdom authority. Social and economic status was of no importance, but rather their hunger and thirst to know Jesus.

And Jesus has turned none of us away. We have lives filled with the abundance of His grace and mercy, and as seasoned women, we are to do what we see Him doing. We are to look on those struggling, whether with or without earthly means and be filled with compassion. We are to advocate for them, mentor them, even sacrifice for them.

We have a mandate to go into all the world and proclaim the gospel. So let us begin with those in our own Jerusalems, and, as GEMs, seek to share grace to the young women all around us.

REFLECTION: WHAT MATTERS MOST

There is no debate that social networking and a near 24/7 preoccupation with media have become the norm today. Unfortunately, social behavior as a whole is tethered by such influences. The advent of the internet has been both a blessing and a curse. Texting, tweeting, and the use of social media now have a dominant influence over this society.

Because of man's propensity toward instant gratification and the "I wanted it yesterday" mentality, today's young people, particularly young women, are caught in the vortex of imitating what they see through the lens of explicit and exploitive music videos, reality TV, and misplaced idolatry of celebrities. Celebrity worship has easily led young people astray, especially if they are looking for purpose and relevance in their lives.

It is natural to wonder how anything else could compete with the manipulative forces in the lives of our young women. But we must not sell ourselves short.

The missing ingredient of their lives is the personal compassion and companionship that we, as GEMs, offer. With the Spirit of Christ, we, as seasoned women, can offer them dignity and a new sense of self-worth. We may become tutors, helping them discover the power of literacy and education. They need to find avenues to learn discipline and teamwork through a sense of community. We should encourage interest in sports and physical health.

Most of all, we are to be the calming voices of reason for a lost girl or young woman. Nothing, truly nothing, is more important than that.

Take time to think of other ways to be agents of change and transformation. Ask, "How would I like to make a difference as a mentor?"

_____
_____
_____
_____
_____
_____
_____
_____
_____
_____
_____
_____
_____
_____
_____
_____
_____
_____
_____
_____
_____
_____
_____
_____
_____
_____
_____
_____

11

RESTORING LOST CONFIDENCE

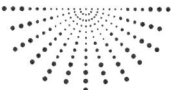

Many people, especially young people, have lost confidence in the Church.

The story is told of a young woman who found herself seated on an airplane beside a gentleman who, as it turned out, was a pastor. She was unhappy. His countenance and demeanor reflected deep unhappiness in life. Finally, the pastor asked if she was all right. This troubled young woman poured out her story of one abusive relationship after the other for several minutes. Her eyes would fill with tears one moment and then change to anger the next.

The pastor listened and, to give her some hope, said to her, "Have you ever tried the Church?"

Her response was filled with disdain, "Why would I do that? Haven't I already been treated badly enough?"

Sadly, tragically, that reflects the opinions of many regarding the church. They may have felt the sting of unkind remarks by the older generation in the community, including the Church. In many cases, they believe that those who profess faith are phonier than faith-filled. The age-old accusation that the church is more about money turns them off. The media that defines the little they know about the world beyond their pain is constantly slaughtering the reputation of believers and heaping ridicule on all but the most liberal religious leaders. At the same time, we have TV shows to make celebrities out of a few cheapening the "gospel" and reducing it to "if it feels good to you, it must be good for you."

Our young women are held in the grip of a world that distorts the truth and leaves them with nothing to see and hear except the mantras of materialism and pleasure. Even though their impulses are to seek such things, they know from experience that those things are nearly always beyond their reach or temporary at best.

The endless quest for pleasure and things blinds them to all else, and many abandon their search for truth and meaning. As a result, the spiritual seed within them becomes the latest victim of spiritual abortion. If we are not attentive, we can easily miss the chance to mentor these young women and point them toward God's purpose for their lives.

If we, as seasoned women, will stand together, we can become a force of faith that calls others to seek God despite the distraction of human frailties and the trials of life. On the other hand, if the younger women cannot discover who they are or who they are, they will continue to struggle.

With the prevailing image of the Church as irrelevant and unwelcoming, our young women see no reason to look to the church. Only as the people of God get off their pews, step beyond the four walls of their comfort zone, and build a new division of love and care, those lost to the gospel are virtually abandoned to the destructive lure of the world.

When the seasoned woman steps into a mentoring role, young women discover that they do not have to face temptations, sinful situations, or moral challenges alone. Instead, with someone at their side, they can begin to make healthy choices that set the trajectory of their lives.

God is love. He does his works through love that elevates us out of the valleys of despair and death and places us on a path of righteousness and truth. In His love, He will never leave us nor forsake us.

The battles we face daily do not ultimately belong to us; they belong to the Lord. Young women are out here fighting over things, people, and possessions without knowing why they do what they do. They need the answers. They need us.

Everybody wants respect and love, but because of the unimaginable deceptions and rejection they have faced, our young women feel like that kind of love is out of reach. Their lives are filled with outbreaks of violence, oppression, suffering, misery, and depression. And their families and friends are battling with the same demons.

They see a hurting world and don't understand why God allows bad things to happen.

They desperately need to discover a whole new reality. They need to see life with fresh eyes and become aware that they have choices. They need women of God to be honest with them and become newly equipped for life by positive modeling. Instead of the piety and hypocrisy they have so commonly faced, they need the honesty that a mentor will provide them. The image of faux faith needs to be replaced with the authentic life of a faith relationship with God and those who truly follow Him.

The testimony of an honest, authentic woman that will draw them to the Savior. Revelations 12:11 declares that "they overcame him because of the blood of the Lamb, and because of the word of their testimony." "They" in that verse points to those who have genuinely chosen to live under the authority of Christ, who is the Lamb of God. His sacrifice and the word of our testimony of His grace makes us victors and paves the way for those who we touch by grace to become overcomers as well.

Just as Jesus went in search of His lost sheep, we as His followers are called to do the same. In the hand of a GEM, the Word of God is the truth that will set the oppressed free.

Grandmothers and seasoned women can no longer sit by and rest on their laurels, watching young women continue to be robbed or destroyed. So, if you are in the winter season of your life, don't allow time to make you feel that you are too old to deal with all that is happening in the world. There is always something you can do. And for those who are concerned about the winter season of life that is coming, stand up with holy defiance and step by faith into the arena, and prevent the spiritual abortion of our young women. I recall the story when God asked Cain about his brother's absence. Cain responded, "Am I my brother's keeper?" His question exposed the heart of Cain's problem. In reality, his question displayed a smugness that revealed Cain's rejection of truth he refused to accept.

Could it be that this question reveals our human tendency to excuse ourselves as well? Does it expose our own gradual failure to be what God designed us to be? Cain had become selfish and grew more and more estranged from the man he was created to be. Can we not see how easy it is to reject those who make us uncomfortable, those who do not share our values or think the way we do?

Are we who sit in our pew week after week so fearful of leaving our familiar pews and comfortable lives that we pass on the privilege of being our "sister's keeper?" Could it be that the answer to all these questions is "yes," and such a thought startles us, causing us to realize we are not what God created us to be?

We face a choice. We can be counted among those who prevent rather than perpetuate the tragedy of spiritual abortions. Our young women are crying out for our help. Let the seasoned woman within you wake up. To awaken to the voice of God calling us to care will be the reason that fallen, hopeless women will wake up, look up, stand up, and live!

REFLECTION: TIPS FROM TONI

Always remember that as a seasoned woman, you are in a perpetual state of learning and growing.

Never, ever decide anything without consulting the Holy Spirit and the Word.

Consistently seek and stand on the Word of God. The Bible is our compass. It is our air and water.

Be sensitive about the women you counsel and mentor, especially regarding where they are spiritually and emotionally, so that you can best speak to their needs. Have compassion, but always speak the truth; never compromise regarding the Word of God.

Allow the following scriptures to be your guide:

> Hereby perceive we the love of God, because he laid down his life for us: and we ought to lay down our lives for the brethren. But whoso hath this world's good, and seeth his brother have need, and shutteth up his bowels of compassion from him, how dwelleth the love of God in him? My little children, let us not love in word, neither in tongue; but in deed and in truth.

> And hereby we know that we are of the truth, and shall assure our hearts before him. For if our heart condemn us, God is greater than our heart, and knoweth all things.

> Beloved, if our heart condemn us not, then have we confidence toward God. And whatsoever we ask, we receive of him, because we keep his commandments, and do those things that are pleasing in his sight. And this is his commandment, that we should believe on the name of his Son Jesus Christ, and love one another, as he gave us commandment. And he

that keepeth his commandments dwelleth in Him, and He in them. And hereby we know that He abideth in us by the Spirit which He hath given us

— I JOHN 3:16-23

12

THE ROLE OF THE SEASONED WOMEN AND GRANDMOTHERS

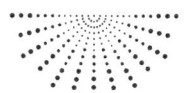

T he Call to Action as Stated in Titus 2:4

Each one of us holds a special place in the heart of God. He longs for us to mature not only in clarity of what we believe but most of all in the rich and ever-growing capacity to know Him. That was, in fact, the Apostle Paul's most pressing desire: "that I may know Him" Philippians 3:10.

In his letter to Titus, this same Paul was prompted by the Spirit to admonish the first-century Christians to be sound in their faith. Paul goes on to speak about the character of believers, noting that their lives should "becomes [having the characteristic of] holiness, not false accusers, not given to much wine and a teacher of good things, teach by example, teach the younger to be discreet, denying ungodliness and worldly lust."

This is an apt description of a seasoned woman or spiritual grandmother. These women possess the character that allows the flow of God's power that activates a spiritual GPS that steers them clear of uncleanness and iniquity, enabling them to become anchored in grace.

Women who follow Christ have been commissioned to share in the global ministry of spreading the gospel. While each GEM can only reach as far as the needy and hungry heart God has placed in their pathways, the combined influence of GEMs at work worldwide generates an impact of hope and grace in the Kingdom of God. Our wisdom and passion touch that girl next door and influence the home and then into her extended family and social network. The reach of a single loving GEM has the potential to spread to a community and beyond.

The wording of Titus 2:4 noted earlier comes from the King James Version of the Bible. The way the New Living Translation (NLT) expresses this passage sheds helpful light that broadens its meaning:

> These older women must train the younger women to love
> their husbands and their children, to live wisely and be
> pure, to work in their homes, to do good, and to be
> submissive to their husbands, then they will not bring
> shame of the word of God.

As shown in the NLT version, God's heart is focused on the family. The impact of living under the influence of grace will be felt throughout the family, like ripples in a spiritual pond.

Ladies, we have a mandate!

As some would suggest, this is not about being nosey, meddlesome, or minding other people's business. Those characteristics have no part in a life intended to exhibit holiness. But the Lord wants us to invest our time, energy, and spiritual fortitude to lead others to live spiritually fit and proper lives. Surrendered to God, our wisdom and caring will reflect Christ to those around us.

Just think of it: as young women struggle through life, your wisdom may be the catalyst that causes someone to overcome life's challenges. But, unfortunately, in the face of today's challenges, it appears that this mission has lost momentum.

At the first-century church, the apostle Paul wrote to Titus that a woman's place consisted of taking care of her family. If she was widowed or unmarried, she served in the synagogue.

So how do Paul's directives to the first-century Church apply to the women in our times?

Today, women are more autonomous. They successfully manage their homes as well as working eight-hour jobs. As a result, on the one hand, women have become a driving force to be reckoned with by breaking down walls, stigmas, and barriers of the past. But, on the other hand, the busy-ness of life, that increased obligations women bear outside of family life has in some cases cast a fog over the plight of others in need and left the calling on the shelf, set aside for "someday" that never seems to come.

We must always look at the Word to discover what the original impact of any passage was meant to have on its listeners. Paul was a learned man, and he knew the characteristics of his society.

Women of that day were not second-class citizens, as some suggest. On the contrary, they were blessed with the capacity to nurture and care in measures that men generally are not. Women were influential in the ministry of Paul himself, and his words were meant to point out that the Church should understand the immense value that women believers provided for the Church.

The role of women to nurture and instruct starting in the home is often minimized mistakenly so. Unlike our culture today, cultural value structures saw strength and stability as centered on the nuclear family. The family name, the progeny of that family line, and the family's cohesiveness as it grew depended on the values and depth of training children received at home. The definitive figure of that hope and expectation was the place and competency of the mother. Women were not devalued in those days, even if their roles were defined differently in our culture today.

In Paul's instructions for the family in Ephesians 5:21, he clearly says that husbands and wives are to submit to each other. That means that each is to value the worth of the other above their own. And it is the worth and value of women that Paul addresses in Titus.

Clearly, in our culture today, we face different social challenges. Indeed, the overt effort in our culture to objectify women as objects of fleshly desires, no matter their many mantras to the contrary, is unequivocally damaging to a woman's worth. That is why the Church must not look through the eyes of our culture but the eyes of our Savior. We are to see each other as He sees us and value each other as He values us. Anything less is simply outside of a Biblical standard for His people.

The wisdom of mature, seasoned women is one of the most powerful and significant keys to empower this generation's success and the stability of the next. Conversely, a lack of wisdom, education, or guidance for our young women is a glaring testament to society's demise.

But if the light of compassion and grace is dimmed in the Church, the results could be devastating both for the future of the Church and certainly for those who search for hope.

A failed mission can only happen in the absence of a vision. An absent vision abandons a whole generation of young women to hopelessness.

So, we now ask difficult questions: 'Is the church failing in its mission? And why?

Perhaps part of the answer comes from the significant shift in the role of women during the last few decades. As women have become a more active part of the workforce, they have found new avenues of fulfillment. They have experienced successes and the energy of accomplishments in a variety of fields. Over the last few generations, the vision of greater achievements has gained momentum and become all-consuming during this transition.

In previous generations of GEMs, the primary role of these women of faith was centered in the home; and as much as some may suggest, the answer is not to turn back the clock. The contributions that women are bringing to society cannot be denied. The suggestion that the professional role of women should be subordinated to the familial role is based on a faulty assumption that this is an either-or situation.

Looking at the great commission, we sometimes miss a key ingredient. In our English rendition of Matthew 28:19-20, the original Greek has been translated as a command: Go, Make disciples, Baptize and Teach. The Greek, however, reads: In your going, make disciples, baptize and teach. The only word in those verses that is not a command is "Go."

God made us active participants in society, so we are people on the go by our nature. Some may go next door. Others reach across town as part of the job market. Still, others reach further into the business community or even across social and cultural barriers. And all of this occurs because we are on the go.

The command of Christ is "go ahead and go; be busy; engage in whatever facet of society you find yourself, but wherever that leads you, the mission is the task that took you there, but rather to use that arena as a place to share grace and compassion. So, wherever we go, in whatever role, that is your place of ministry, the place in which you make disciples.

As much as that applies to men as well as women, our focus here is the renewal of a vision in the life of women to become GEMs to the daughters and sisters in your life, whether that is at home or next door or your "second home" where you have been entrusted with a broader mission.

In addition to the change of the workplace, there is also the natural transition of age. As we get older, there is a matter of our energy level. We find ourselves going less. But age should not dull the vision. On the contrary, it may necessitate a change of venue and a narrowing of our reach as a pragmatic measure. Still, the mission and the vision must remain vivid and always present tense.

Another issue is that today grandmothers are often much younger than in the past. Some take on the role of a grandparent in their thirties. Unfortunately, our children are having children, even in some cases in their early teens. This family dynamic can be a challenge but facing such a struggle is much easier to overcome with the right GEM in their lives. Perhaps young grandmothers need to be awakened to this vision so they can begin to share their wisdom and faith in the immediate arena of the family and be available for other families with the same.

Yet another reason the vision may wane may be the struggle some women have with shame, embarrassment, or guilt we carry from our past. None of us can escape these issues because we all have things in our history that cause us to feel unworthy or not qualified to be messengers of grace. We fear that someone will find out what we have done or not done and think less of us. Sadly, such feelings rob us of the joy of sharing how the grace of God administered by someone who cared enough for us changed our lives. If any lingering shame or guilt remains, even that experience can become a living lesson to others that grace is available to help us grow more each day. Every day of our lives, we need to seek a fresh touch of grace.

Nothing will speak more of credibility and authenticity to the next generation than raw encounters with those times when we, the mentors, openly live out our own need for grace. When we share grace in real-time and in real-life situations and do so in faith and humility, our younger generation looks on and realizes we are for real. Few things we can see will declare grace more than the evidence of grace embraced anew in our own lives.

Our task of transferring what measure of wisdom we have with others is never as strong as when our pursuit and embrace of grace is transparent. Our mistakes can be as impactful as our victories.

As GEMs, we do not want, in any way, to deny the next generation of their spiritual heritage. However, we could argue that we do not understand the problems of today's young women, and in one sense, that would be true. What they face today may not be familiar to us. Their struggles may not be the same as what we had to deal with in our day. We know that in these troubling times, they will make mistakes, but in the end, many of them will be the same mistakes we made, only shaped differently on this day.

But regardless of the problem or the time frame in which they are experienced, God is the problem-solver as much for them as He was and continues to be for us.

REFLECTION

Titus 2:4 must be both a pronouncement as well as an assignment. Living these truths is an ongoing process. It is a daily decision to embrace its reality because our mission does not stop when our young women come of age. We are called to be there for those who need us as long as God gives us the opportunity. Wisdom is ageless. It will grow as a person grows. Wisdom and knowledge are interconnected. Wisdom is discerning, looking behind the obvious, and seeing the divine component of life's problem-solving. Wisdom offers peaceful solutions and stability and assists in strategies and decision-making abilities.

It might help us remember that wisdom is the centerpiece of the first section of the Proverbs. And wisdom is always mentioned as "Wisdom." The pronoun for Wisdom is "she." Scholars tell us that the second person of the Trinity who later came as Christ to be our Savior is the One who is being portrayed cryptically as Wisdom. How significant that the one we are to trust in life, this Wisdom is presented to us a "she!"

Grandmothers and seasoned women have a unique and unusual place in God's plan. They provide wisdom because they have chosen to pause for contemplation in the presence of God, sitting and thinking, reaching levels of understanding that hold significant blessings for others. Their wisdom impacts every aspect of our lives.

These lessons didn't happen in a day. Life lessons are passed down from others, as my grandmother taught me.

Nothing is, therefore, more important than our relationship with God, whose very nature is the essence of Wisdom. We have experienced how God moves in our lives in that relationship, bringing us into our blessings. Therefore, we are seasoned enough to teach young women, as stated in Psalm 27:14, how to wait on the Lord and be of good courage in any situation.

A young lady who needed a GEM shared the following story with me. She was a single mother known for having a less than pleasant encounter with a seasoned woman in her church. But I need to add that the young lady is intuitive, intelligent, and very independent.

She shared the following with me:

> Some seasoned women tend to get a little intimidated and show signs of jealousy because of my looks, wisdom, and intellect. Because I was young, this particular sister at the church treated me as if I needed only to listen and not speak. She was unwilling to embrace the simple fact that I had a few questions. When I did question her about something, her response was offensive. She cut me off and treated me as if I did not know what I was talking about. When I saw her the next Sunday, she did not want to speak to me. This led to her closing the door of communication. It left me feeling like I had done something wrong.

This experience could have affected her negatively thinking about Titus 2:4, but fortunately, it did not. I asked this young woman if this affected how she felt about all the women in the church. She shared the following:

> I still need these women in my life, though some may feel a little intimidated by my knowledge, wit, and skills which I have to offer. We still need one another. My grandmother recently died, and we were close. I miss that connection. I was raised to respect my elders. They are the jewels that carry years of wisdom.

This is an example of one young lady's experience with a Christian woman. She assumed she could reach out and have a void filled, an emptiness that occurred at her grandmother's death with whom she was so close. Maybe you know someone who has the same story.

We must begin to see ourselves as Titus 2:4 women so young women can experience love.

Take time to think about ways to be more sensitive when approached by someone who needs your understanding and care. Have I listened enough? How can I be a better GEM?

13

THE ORIGINAL SEASONED GEMS AND YOU

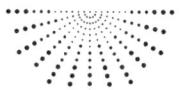

JOANNA, MARY MAGDALENE, AND MARY, MOTHER OF JESUS

J oanna, Mary Magdalene, and Mary, the mother of Jesus, were seasoned women. They experienced challenges, suffered unknown agony, and were graced with unimaginable blessings.

I came across a devotional quotation which states, "God became what we are so that we might become what He is." This quote intends to point out that Christ entered our world as one of us, fully incarnational so that we too can live incarnationally among others. He did not come alongside us because we deserve it, nor because we have earned it. Instead, he has set us free by the power of a love divine and utterly amazing.

This statement reminds me of a wealthy woman in the Bible named Joanna, which in Hebrew means "the Lord is Grace." Through God's grace, she was healed of infirmities. From the time she was healed, her relationship with Christ was firm. Joanna showed her gratitude for her physical restoration and salvation by ministering to Jesus from her substance from that day on. She was a woman of hospitality who took care of Jesus and the disciples. She honored the Lord with what she had, which exemplified the grace of giving.

Joanna would be known today as a woman of God who also was a savvy businesswoman. She practiced service, devotion, and obedience regarding the things of God. She went from rags to riches in her journey to spiritual salvation. Joanna went from not knowing Jesus to becoming consumed by Him. She practiced service, devotion, and obedience regarding the things of God.

Think about how much God has given out of His grace and love for us. As we share, we become a blessing to others, just as Joanna did. God's grace is sufficient in all that we do for others as we take on the character of Christ. Joanna doesn't have thirty-nine chapters written about her. Still, within the few verses of scripture in the book of Luke, her story unfolds in various verses describing a profound impact her ministry had on the gospel of God's grace and love.

This wife of Chuza was one of the first women given special mention in the Gospels along with Mary Magdalene; Mary, the mother of Jesus; Mary, the mother of James and John; Mary, the wife of Clopas; and Salome, the mother of James and John.

Mary Magdalene struggled with what would be known today as "spiritual oppression." Christ delivered her from her deep inner turmoil. This act was the catalyst that led her to follow Him and devote herself to His Service before and after His death on the cross. Her passion was to share the Gospel and help women who had experienced struggle and loss.

Mary, the mother of Jesus, was a young woman chosen by God the Father to bring Jesus Christ, the Son of God, into the world. Just think of it. Scripture lets us know that Mary was a young woman. Biblical scholars share that Mary was between the ages of fifteen and seventeen. Think of the faith and maturity that was needed for her to go forth and fulfill her purpose. She became a loving mother raising the Son of God, growing into a woman of strength, discipline, and substance who endured the agony of witnessing her Son's death on the cross.

Pause for a moment and think about the women who had nurtured Mary in those few short years before she bore the Christ child. Yet, she did not reach such spiritual depth in so few years without significant companionship with others modeled wisdom and grace in her life.

These three women – Joanna, Mary Magdalene, Mary the Mother of Jesus – and two other previously mentioned women discovered the empty tomb. These women could be referred to as the Original New Testament GEMS.

If you have a relationship with Christ, you too can walk as those women did. They showed their gratitude by sharing what they had with others because of the impact of Jesus' life on them.

All good, strong relationships take time and commitment. Our daily prayers and worship of the Lord are essential. When I say "praise and worship," I am not primarily focused on a Sunday morning music program. "Praise and worship" should fill and characterize our lives of fellowship with Christ. Every act offers worship and expression of our praise and gratitude for His presence and grace. Such a life becomes a living epistle, written in our influence of grace in others' lives. Such a life is about being an ambassador of His grace.

Think about how much of God's grace and love that's invested in you, and as you dare to share, you multiply those blessings to others. The women we have noted did just that.

God powerfully used each one of these women. Their lives were devoted to Him, and His grace was poured out to others through them.

Do we not all have much to share out of the abundant blessing and the wealth of grace we have received from God? Have we not experienced His goodness in great measure that we can now overflow into others? If His grace is sufficient for our lives, that would include our calling to touch others with that grace.

Is there something preventing you from sharing the blessing of the Lord with others? What is blocking the flow of grace in your life and preventing you from being God's GEMs?

These women endured incredible hurt, pain, ridicule, shame, attack on their reputations, and unfounded hearsay. But they did not lose their faith in God, and they maintained their righteous character.

REFLECTION: WHO ARE YOU?

Each of the three women, Joanna, Mary Magdalene, and Mary the mother of Jesus, were examples of everyday women. Today, one was considered a wise homemaker, one a mature single woman who had known many trials. Perhaps she would have been considered a product or casualty of the urban jungle of her day. One was a teenage girl who would have been seen as an unwed, pregnant teenager in today's world. Yet, all were mightily transformed through an amazing encounter with a Holy God.

Which one are you? Who do you closely resonate with? Maybe each one reminds you of a different part of your life. What attributes of these women can you relate to? How did the Savior change you? How is He continuing to bless your life?

_____
_____
_____
_____
_____
_____
_____
_____
_____
_____
_____
_____
_____
_____
_____
_____

14
KNOW YOURSELF

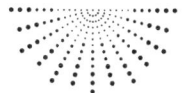

YOUR ATTITUDE, WALK, AND
RELATIONSHIP WITH CHRIST

We discussed some wonderful, seasoned women in the last chapter. Hopefully, these women and their devotion to Christ spurs us to focus more clearly on our mission, the purposes, and the goals that fill our vision. Perhaps their examples become the catalysts for us to renew our commitment to being light in the lives of young women, lovingly walking with them as they face their struggles and weaknesses, and fears.

As we listen to those in need, we permit them to speak openly and transparently. Such a healing relationship will enable them to develop the traits of faith-filled lives that lead to:

That kind of companionship will open the door for them to begin discovering the grace and spiritual attributes they need:

- Loving and honoring their marriages
- Nurturing their families, whether the fathers are in the home or not
- Respecting themselves
- Practicing financial discipline and responsibility
- Having spiritual awareness

- Discovering the power and wonder in the praise and worship of prayer
- Embracing a deep desire to honor God by adopting good health practices and maintaining mental wellness

These qualities cannot be stressed enough.

And the best way to help these young women to make such shifts in their perspective is for us to listen, listen, and listen some more; land by being transparent examples and role models. Listening with a loving heart and transparent modeling are the essential ingredients in becoming a conduit of change in their lives.

I John 4:12 says that "If we love one another, God dwelleth in us, and His love is perfected in us." No one is perfect in this life. Perfection in our performance is not a reality, so in Christ, do your best, be your best, and this is enough.

But, in that verse, there is a truth that comes first, reminding us that "No man hath seen God at any time." By implication, the love for one another is the answer to seeing God. Thus, the verse could read, in an amplified, commentary-like wording, as:

> Nobody has ever seen God, but when you love one another,
> evidencing the God who lives in us, His love in us is
> perfected and is then perfectly able to do as He has planned
> all along: people will finally be able to see God in your life
> of love.

The ideas of (1) no one seeing God and (2) our love for one another are not linked by accident. They belong together. And, truthfully, if our future GEMs, and for that matter, our current GEMs, could grasp the connection in that verse, it would be all they need to be the guides and mentors our younger women need.

To live out the truth of that verse in real ways would overshadow any of our human inadequacies in pursuit of our mission, including:

- Criticism (a reaction that causes us to tell them how they should act instead of teaching them to understand the why of their choices)
- Takeover (the assumption that you must "take control" instead of instilling confidence that they can make good decisions)
- Comparison or competition (a trap that only measures success in comparison to one's own expectations or the performance of another, instead of by the gentleness of grace)
- Falsehood (Be gentle and sincere, authentic. They are not fools; just young.)

Even for young GEMs, you are the glue that will hold the young ladies together. As we walk in partnership with Christ, by His grace, we will be His vessel of grace whether someone needs counsel or simply a loving shoulder to cry on.

Matthew 4:45-46 reminds us that the servant who, when the master comes home and finds his servant faithfully doing what he was entrusted to do, will be "blessed." Jesus' words here do not include any reference to the servant's productivity, only his faithfulness. The lesson is clear. We are blessed for simply faithfully doing what the Lord asks us to do.

You are here to have a meaningful life and to love and serve people, and in doing so, we are serving Christ. The Church is a gathering place for souls to receive grace to grow from Godly instruction. It is a place where pastors preach and teach the Word of God that guides us through the maze of life's decisions and choices. It is a place of healing, a place of refreshing. How can this happen? It happens as seasoned Christian women embrace their Titus 2:4 assignment.

There has been some criticism leveled from time to time that certain grandmothers and seasoned women are mean-spirited and selfish, have a hateful complaining attitude, and are uncaring should those of the younger set fail and fall. Sadly, that is sometimes the case, usually when a GEM is experiencing her own hidden hurt and pain and has no one to come alongside her to help her deal with life.

The hurt and pain in the life of a GEM can and often is gauged by her attitude towards others. For example, sharing uncaring, even negative thoughts about someone is one symptom. Other comments that reveal a problem would include:

"This is who I am. If you don't like it, too bad."
"It is not my problem. I have enough of my own."
"I am grown. I do what I want to do when I want to do it and how I want to do it."
"I am too old to change now."
"I take care of me and mine. You mind your own business and take care of your children."

Does any of this sound familiar? All you hear is "I," "I," "I," and more "I's." Some GEMs suffer from an "I" disease.

Ask yourself, "How did she get to this point? Is this the image that represents Christ? Do I reflect the attributes of the woman described in Titus 2:4?" How can I avoid this kind of pitfall?

Many GEMs are dealing with a long list of burdens. Un-forgiveness and past pain create a wall. Our actions come with a price and are on the front stage to be seen by our young. They watch us, listen to how we respond to situations, review our behavior constantly, imitate and practice, and even go as far as acting out the way they have seen us act. Sometimes, they even think they are being cute. They watch and learn. That may not be our intention, but when we are not healed from our past, we are in danger of passing on our baggage to others.

The afflicted do not and cannot heal because they cannot trust others no matter the setting, whether within the church's four walls or in their day-to-day lives.

Does your soul still reek of old lies from yesteryears that have a grip on you? Are you still holding on to unhelpful practices and habits? Are you still trying to recapture your youth by dressing as 'they' dress?

Our young women need you to heal from the wounds of your past so that they can receive the wisdom and Godliness that is being stifled within you due to your unresolved issues. They are looking for women who portray the character and reputation that the preacher teaches about. They don't need hypocrisy; they need spiritual wisdom and knowledge that teaches them to be an overcomer through Christ.

We have the power within called the Holy Spirit. The Holy Spirit gives us the power to overcome the hurt of our past, even the hurts from the church, allowing us to provide guidance and mentorship to our young women and allowing them to fulfill their places and positions of greatness. I once heard someone say that "our arms are too short to box with God." Release your true self so God can break you out of the prison mindset you have been battling for so many years.

Past pain will keep you hostage. Your mind will remain captive to torment, blocking you from living a victorious life. The ripple effect is the negative effect those actions would have on our young GEMs.

Here is a conversation I had with a young GEM. Her observation is profound. She asked, "What happened to healing?"

Is this how we are seen through the eyes of the younger?

The church is known as the place for sick souls, where God can heal the sick of heart, sick of mind, and sick of body. People forget where they came from and what sins they have overcome with God's blessings and grace. They become so high and mighty that they shun and cast stones at those trying to find their way. How can healing occur when everyone is hurting and, in turn, hurting others?

Hurt people hurt people. Hurting GEMs have to heal from their pain so that they can help the younger women heal, too. The younger women are hurting in ways that they cannot express except through self-mutilation, bad behavior, and disrespect of all kinds. They have no respect for others because no one gives them any. And obviously, they have no respect for themselves. No one has guided them or shown them how to respect themselves. When they can love themselves, they will learn to respect themselves, and this process will help them love and respect others. Love heals and covers a multitude of sins and is the main thing lacking in our churches, homes, and communities.

So how does a GEM break this stronghold? God has given us free will. You can decide to do right or do wrong. The final decision resides within you. The answer can be found in 2 Corinthians 10:3-8:

> For though we walk in the flesh, we do not war after the flesh:
> For the weapons of our warfare are not carnal, but mighty
> through God to the pulling down of strong holds;) Casting
> down imaginations, and every high thing that exalteth itself
> against the knowledge of God, and bringing into captivity
> every thought to the obedience of Christ; And having in a
> readiness to revenge all disobedience, when your obedience
> is fulfilled. Do ye look on things after the outward
> appearance? if any man trust to himself that he is Christ's,
> let him of himself think this again, that, as he is Christ's,
> even so are we Christ's. For though I should boast
> somewhat more of our authority, which the Lord hath given
> us for edification, and not for your destruction, I should not
> be ashamed:

We have the authority. When we cast down every thought, we cast down thoughts of envy, jealousy, gossip, nervous breakdowns, and depression. These problems come to wreak havoc and destruction in our lives, but God says if we take on the mind of Christ, we level the playing field, and we become winners.

Paul is clear, problems are for our benefit: "For though I should boast somewhat more of our authority, which the Lord hath given us for edification, and not for your destruction, I should not be ashamed. We are not to be ashamed" - 2 Corinthians 10:8.

When you love people, all signs of falseness, pretense, manipulation, and being mean-spirited will dissipate, ending the spread of negativity. Some of the enemy's tricks can take place within the walls of the church, leading believers down a path of subtle destruction. If not handled correctly, this poison will then take on another face, one that will cause one to feel that they are going through a spiritual exercise Sunday after Sunday, placating people instead of being real, "Having a form of godliness, but denying the power thereof: from such turn away - 2 Timothy 3:5.

This negativity grows in our hearts; ultimately, teaching families to do the same from the pulpit to the back door. Our younger women suffer. It is a sad day when a young woman loses interest in the Church because the members begin to believe the negative behaviors they see are a representation of Christ.

Forgive yourself and forgive others who may have hurt you in the past or even today. Leave hurt behind; t may make you physically sick if you don't. Do not babysit your pain.

There was a time when I went through my divorce, and I put my hurt and pain to rest in a nice little crib. I held divorce and rocked it to sleep. When it cried, I gave it a bottle and fed it, gave it a pacifier to keep it quiet. I nurtured it and loved it, always justifying its presence. The pain was comfortable right where I put it, warm and asleep, and I did not want anyone to wake up or disturb my baby, my pain, or my hurt. Why? Because I didn't want to hear pain cry out the word "wrong," "forgive," "apologize."

I just wanted to be right, so I kept nursing the baby. I found that it is just like a baby crying when going through the healing of pain and past hurts. After a while, the baby doesn't need the bottle anymore. It's growing up, and it requires different food to grow. This is when you choose to keep feeding the pain, thereby making it stronger to control your life.

It's time to change your diet. Switch from milk to meat. Feed on something of substance to sustain you and make you stronger, the Word of God.

As you get stronger and begin to heal, you will not cry over that situation again because you have learned a valuable lesson. And you're healed. It's a good thing the Holy Spirit comes to test you and disturb your baby. It will not even faze you because, over time, God took away the pain. God has done this for me. He will do it for you.

Often, young ladies who share their stories with me are hurting and in need of some guidance. We may be called upon to be transparent and honest. Just think, there are young women out there who do not have anyone helping them through some of the most complex trials in their lives. You may be counted as one of the few who was fortunate enough to have someone to be your sounding board. Others do not. What kind of decisions are they making? We can do this one young lady at a time. A person interested in making an impact in the lives of others is also making an impact by saving families.

The Bible says we should not take anything or anyone for granted.

A good reputation is better than a fat bank account; your death date tells more than your birthdate - Ecclesiastes 7:1.

Remember the "dash," that line that lies between your date of birth and the date of your death. That little dash covers your sojourn on this earth.

REFLECTION: WHAT ABOUT YOU?

Were you at one time in such a place? Misunderstood and rejected? Were you exposed to a bad example of what a woman of God is supposed to be? How did it affect you? Did it cause you to run from God or to Him? Are you still on the journey back to God? If so, it is time to embrace the process of releasing the bad memories and embracing what the Savior has waiting for you.

I've forgiven:

_____

_____

_____

_____

_____

I have released:

_____

_____

_____

_____

_____

I have embraced:

_____

_____

_____

_____

_____

_____

_____

THE IMPORTANCE OF ENCOURAGEMENT

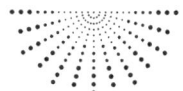

A s I hold meaningful conversations with younger women, they tell me they would love to be mentored by grandmothers or older seasoned women. But unfortunately, they have witnessed some troubling behaviors. In addition, they had a few bad experiences with older women discussed later in this chapter.

Deep down inside, they long to have older women in their lives that they may look up to. Many times, what is forgotten is that there is someone always watching what we do. What types of examples are being set? They do not want to see older women act the way they do. They are thrown off balance when they witness us demonstrating a poor example of womanhood. They see older women -- who should be serving as examples - gossiping, backbiting, and partying harder than they do.

If we are following the ways of Christ, this discussion should not be necessary. But, if we are going to teach these young women how to love and respect themselves and expect them to listen to us, there are things that we must stop doing that cause them to question our behaviors and Christian walk.

This takes me to a story about a young single mother I know who was offended in the church. She relayed the following experience to me:

> "Church people smile in your face, say common phrases, and all the while, they would talk about you behind your back while hanging in small groups." She vowed never to go back because, "at least in the world I know what to expect, people are people in the world; they don't come with many hidden faces."

She experienced feelings of hurt and rejection. She needed GEMs with whom she could be real, someone without a critical or judgmental spirit. She needed someone who would not look down on her, explain her confusion, and help her manage adverse treatment by church members.

When things of this nature happen, it affects the woman and her family, especially her children. Incidents such as these often turn young people off and away from the church. Unfortunately, this young mother left the church to become again ensnared by the cares and traps of this world, looking for love and acceptance in all the wrong places. There is no greater pain than church hurt. This can destroy a young woman's view of Christ, creating low self-esteem along with a host of other problems.

Wouldn't Jesus have gone after her? Of course! She needed a GEM who could have provided absolute transparency and love. You don't have to tell young people all your buried secrets or hidden parts of your life. That is entirely up to you. Transparency must be exercised with discernment.

And there is a way of being transparent without coming across as though you were perfect. Church hurt can be the worst pain someone can suffer. I heard a preacher once say, "the church is the hospital for sick souls."

And base things of the world, and things which are despised,
hath God chosen, yea, and things which are not, to bring to
nought things that are: that no flesh should glory in his
presence. But of him are ye in Christ Jesus, who of God is
made unto us wisdom, and righteousness, and
sanctification, and redemption

— I CORINTHIANS 1:28-31

We nevertheless must line up according to the Word of God and be about our Father's business. It is time to change young women's opinions about the church and its people. We cannot turn back the hands of time to retrieve what has been lost because of our decisions.

Embrace the decisions and mistakes you've made in the past. You have already overcome them. Use them as examples to help younger women avoid the pitfalls and consequences of making bad decisions and choices. You have no reason to feel guilty about questionable decisions you made throughout your life before coming to salvation.

Time waits for no one, and if we have professed holiness and are walking righteously, Christ can restore what the locust has stolen, supplying us with love, wisdom, and guidance that can be freely shared.

A powerful movement could be born if seasoned women everywhere were to do this. If we leave our past in the past, we will help younger women realize their dreams and hidden potential. They are waiting for us to guide them to discover or recover their gifts and talents. When one of these young women finally opens her heart to trust us, we are to guide her delicately and lovingly toward a heart for God, giving her the tools she needs to live a victorious life.

You never know what a young lady's story is until you get to know her. God may send you someone who is being abused, living on the streets, or hustling. Some young women may live in what would be considered a wonderful environment but may also face the same challenges of drugs and drinking. Such problems do not belong just to the poor but are a challenge for individuals in all walks of life.

You may even be faced with a life and death situation. For instance, a young lady may be on the verge of deciding to have an abortion or contemplating suicide. Those young ladies desperately need a real friend. We are equipped through the grace of God to stand in the gap with them, help them, literally to rescue them from the jaws of hell.

If God has placed someone in your path, become a mentor or friend to them. Each one entrusted to you needs you to remind her that her life is precious and that her Father in Heaven loves her.

For the one who is pregnant without a husband, or the baby's father in the picture, become her family. Let her know that you will be by her side as she chooses life for her child. Whether she has already chosen to keep and raise her child, opted for adoption, or has had an abortion, just love her, especially if she has undergone an abortion, because she will experience so many emotions, some that may not surface for a while.

We should be the first line of care. We are to be someone who loves, cares for, and prays with those young women who are struggling and hurting.

Let us be prepared to meet these young women at their specific points of need. Don't examine their situation through the cloudy lens of the world's standards. We are in an awesome position to show the love of Christ in the most horrific times of their young lives. As morally wrong and carnal as we feel their decisions may be, we cannot turn our backs on them because Christ did not turn his back on us. Abandoning them can lead them to make worse decisions, bringing more harm to them and the people who share their lives.

Our responsibility is to share the truths of Kingdom living, allowing them to see an alternative to their past as they discover the mind of the King through the Word of God and the grace we share. As young women build their spiritual muscles, things will become more evident. They will make informed decisions based on scripture that forever can change their future.

> Know ye not that they which run in a race run all, but one
> receiveth the prize? So run, that ye may obtain

> — I CORINTHIAN 9:24

As this occurs, their relationship with Christ begins to develop, becoming personal and stable. The role of this spiritual Grandmother goes from 'occasional mentor' to trusted confidant and friend. As written in 1 Corinthians 3:7, "One may plant, but God gives the increase." So then neither is he that planteth anything, neither he that watereth; but God that giveth the increase."

My grandmother walked the walk and talked the talk, through God's grace given to GEMs to use their wisdom to build a strong foundation in younger women. Each seasoned woman masterfully takes each experience and builds on it by helping another patiently, lovingly, mindfully, and informationally. A young woman who has received the wisdom of seasoned women will build a foundation of endurance and receive the personal ability to stand in their worth. You will feel enabled, empowered, and equipped to walk in the love of those seasoned women who helped you along the way.

Young women must be willing to be taught and to listen. Hebrews 13:16-18 states, "Obey them that rule over you, and submit yourselves: for they watch for your souls, as they must give account, that they may do it with joy, and not with grief; for that is unprofitable for you."

At this point, I do not want to sound like I was flawless. I, too, made decisions, some of them utterly reckless. My grandmother would have turned over in her grave. I, too, experienced disappointments, fears, and rejections. Yet, somehow, during those times, all the many words of wisdom from seasoned women came together as keys to help unlock the grace of God in my life. After many trials, defeats, and victories, I discovered a particular rhythm to life through all of that. I realized that the things I believed to be negative experiences molded me to become the seasoned woman I am today, helping other young women build a strong foundation in their lives.

REFLECTION: ENCOURAGING HER, ENCOURAGING YOU

There is nothing like beautiful words of encouragement to lift a person's spirits. So, write as many statements of encouragement or affirmation that you know will lift your mentee as well as serve as an encouragement to you!

1. _____
2. _____
3. _____
4. _____
5. _____
6. _____
7. _____
8. _____
9. _____
10. _____
11. _____
12. _____
13. _____
14. _____
15. _____
16. _____
17. _____
18. _____
19. _____
20. _____

ARE YOU READY?

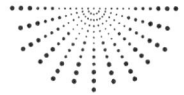

W e are designed to be spiritual guides for young women, bringing kingdom standards and principles to them that will give them understanding. Then, as they mature through the Word of God, the Holy Spirit will provide them with a deeper understanding of who they are and how He is bringing them closer to Christ.

Can you imagine what would happen to our young women if the grandmothers and seasoned women failed to embrace their assignments? Think for a moment: is there someone that comes across your mind as you read this? What do you have to give out of your reservoir of wisdom? They need what you have to accomplish a greater good in their lives.

In my research, I found one reason many grandmothers or 'seasoned women' do not move in their assignments. They have not been taught to fill this place of calling, even within their churches. The following excerpt from the book Vintage Church by Pastor Mark of Mars Hill Church may add some direction.

A few billion people worship Jesus Christ every week and do so in the church as the church. Yet, if you walk into various churches and ask the people who comprise that church what the word 'church' means, the odds are that you will get either a blank stare or a series of conflicting definitions. Sadly, this is even true [of] their pastors. I asked various pastors of some of America's largest churches - godly men and dear friends - if they have a working definition of the church. Not one of them did. Instead, they confessed they were giving their lives to building something for which they did not even have a clear definition.

This is an insightful opinion on the misdirection of a missing sense of purpose in many church members' lives, especially the confusion common in modern-day churches. But unfortunately, it is not the standard for every Church.

The Church, ultimately, is the Body of Christ, a body of believers who experience a community that encourages, lifts, supports, and loves one another. The "Church" has often been compared to a hospital for sick souls needing the Great Physician, Jesus Christ, who can heal where no medical doctor can ever touch.

Believers make up the Body of Christ, and as a body, we are called the Church. Therefore, how well a church is performing and how healthy it is can be directly measured by the quality of the people they can train and retain. And that is especially so with seasoned women who hold a lifetime of wisdom.

If we are not receiving direction – you guessed it – the younger women will be spiritually starved out of the pews, returning to a lifestyle familiar to them, a worldly system that has its arms open wide to offer temporal and fleshly delights. This leads to a trail of destruction and a pathway of pain that prohibits the gift that Christ offers - unreserved and unconditional love for all His people.

If only 80 percent of people agree with Pastor Mark's synopsis, here is your opportunity to help young women. Join the ranks of other GEMs who are connecting with the young women in need.

Maybe the Titus 2:4 call that Apostle Paul wrote so clearly and passionately will help you see how your place of importance in the lives of others never ends. Regardless of your age, you are an asset.

2 Timothy 2:21 says that we are to "be a vessel for honor, sanctified and useful for the Master, prepared for every good work."

REFLECTION: TIPS FROM TONI

Many young dreams are waiting to be cultivated and stimulated through interaction with GEMs. The following eight statements of empowerment will help navigate the road to success:

1. Use your leadership skills to equip, support, motivate, and mentor individuals to become all that God wants them to be while under your care.
2. Sit down, listen to their interests, and help them identify their gifts and talents.
3. Help them with the research that will direct them to information that best matches the goals that they wish to achieve.
4. With spiritual passion, share why you are a Christian.
5. Teach the importance of expressing and sharing the compassion of humanity, community interaction, the needs of others, volunteerism, and positively taking part in everyday life issues that aid in the overall health of mankind.
6. Be involved. The young want you to meet them at their point of need. They also need you to translate ideas in many ways so that they can hear the truth and feel loved individually.
7. Love unconditionally. The high holy standard of unconditional love is contagious. As they experience genuine love, the younger women will be stronger in their lives and relationships. Strong connections will lead to strong families, allowing the future to be forever changed.
8. Seek the guidance of the Lord continuously. Never make a decision, no matter how small, without consulting Him.

17

TRIBUTES TO GEMS

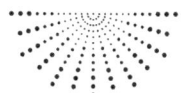

Beautiful Grandmothers that Experienced Life-Changing Challenges, Turbulent Paths, and Jubilant Journeys

Sometimes it just takes the courage to be you and stand out instead of trying to fit in. Through joy, pain, trial, and privation, these women highlighted below rose, made contributions, and in doing so created family tree legacies.

GEM JOAN CRYSTAL PETTIS (MARCH 30, 1939 -)

Joan Pettis is the mother of Reverend Toni Kleckley. Born Joan Sadler, she is the youngest of four children born to a domestic engineer and a minister. Her father worked in a meat plant in Shelbyville, Indiana. She was part of the generation of children who were not that long removed from the institution of slavery. Her family migrated from Carrollton, Kentucky, to Shelbyville, Indiana.

While in Shelbyville, Joan attended the only two-room schoolhouse for African American students. The seating arrangements were in rows according to their grade level. The first-grade students sat in the first row, second graders in the second, and continued to the sixth grade. By the time Joan reached the fourth row, her parents had moved to Indianapolis, Indiana, where she completed her grade school and middle school years.

Joan graduated from Shortridge High School. After graduating from high school, she worked to pay her way through nursing school. She graduated in 1962 as a Licensed Practical Nurse. After 36 years of passionately serving the sick, she retired.

Joan married Raymond Pettis. They had one child, Toni, who became an ordained, licensed minister and entrepreneur.

Joan is a grandmother of two and great-grandmother of six. Her granddaughter Ta'Nia and her grandson Wesley say this about their GEM.

Ta'Nia – "My grandmother means so much to me. She is my treasure, a wonderful, loving person deeply embedded in my heart. I can remember times when I was going through some tough growing pains. Then, she would lovingly embrace me, praying for me in a sweet, unique way while tears were flowing down my face.

I did not understand everything she said at the time, but her spirit, strength, and soul have made me the prayer warrior I am today. I knew then, and know now, that she is still my place of safety. She was my softness when my heart was hardened.

I remember times standing by her in the kitchen helping with baking or cleaning dishes, listening to her stories of our family history. She taught me the difference between real friends and fake friends. Another one of my best GEM moments was seeing her at my high school graduation. I think we both deserved that diploma. LOL – Yeah!!! We made it across the finish line. Mommy Joan, you are my bright star, a compass that always pointed me in the right direction. Just like you, I will always hold my head up, never down. My GEM's life is my example: hard work first, then play, caring for those who are less fortunate, and perseverance through adversity. Even though we are a few hours apart, I try to live a life that honors you and God. Any thought of you makes me smile! I am touched deeply forever by your love. I love you, Mommy Joan, and thank you for everything. You are my GEM."

Wesley – "Mommy Joan, your love is timeless; you are incredible, loving, sophisticated, and powerful in your right. There are so many family memories I could discuss. I remember you sitting on the sideline at football and soccer games and how you came to my karate practices and competitions. You and grandpa would drive over two hours from Indy to support me. It made me happy seeing my family cheering me on by the baseline. I remember how hard I worked at making good grades in school because I knew that you were going to slip me a dollar for every A and fifty cents for every B. Believe it or not, this principle kept me motivated and disciplined me, teaching me to understand that hard work pays off. It's just so much to remember. Let me add, thank you for willfully passing on your life-long lessons to my mother. She has taken your lessons and passed on the values of what you wanted foundationally for this family. And guess what? I'm now teaching the same values to my family.

During my time in the Military, you may have been out of sight but never out of mind. Your letters, cards, and indulgences brought me and the other troop's joy, connection, and comfort. Lesson learned: never give up or give in; follow the still little voice inside me. It will never lead me wrong— and my favorite saying of hers is — see God in all people even if they don't believe in God. Our family commitment to one another has stood the test of time, whether times are good or challenging. These are never bad times; it is in those moments when we want to say "bad" we can embrace God as He educates us with hope and cultivates our maturity. Thank you for your sacrifices. I am forever grateful, and I love you. You are a GEM of a woman."

MARIAN SHIELDS ROBINSON (MAY 30, 1937 -)

Marian Robinson is the mother of former First Lady Michelle Obama. Born Marion Shields, she was the fourth of seven children born to a house painter and a licensed practical nurse. She was one of the many descendants of families that participated in the Great Migration, fleeing the oppression of the South in favor of opportunities in the Northern United States.

Marian was raised and attended school in Chicago, Illinois. Upon graduation, she married Mr. Frasier Robinson, and they had two children, Craig and Michelle. The latter grew up to be the First Lady of the United States of America upon the election of President Barack Obama.

Mrs. Obama has said the following about her mother and the influence she has had on her life:

"My mom is an incredibly intelligent and insightful person about life in general. From the time we could talk, she talked to us endlessly about any and everything with a level of openness and fearlessness that made us believe that we were bright enough to engage with an adult, that we were worthy enough to ask questions and to get serious answers - and she did it with a level of humor. So many times, we were in the midst of getting spanked or disciplined, and she would start cracking up. She taught my brother and me not to take things so seriously; to work hard, but to learn to laugh at situations and laugh at yourself and then to move through it."

SOJOURNER TRUTH (1797 - 1883)

Born a slave, Truth changed her name from Isabella Baumfree in 1843 when she was 46 years old. Some would say she reinvented herself as the women's rights advocate, civil rights activist, and trailblazer she became. With famous works like "Ain't I A Woman?" she became a concrete fixture as a voice for women. She fought for her rights by getting her son back and working tirelessly to uplift her people. As a grandmother, she lived with her two grandsons and her daughter while still advocating to move America forward. Her service will not be soon forgotten.

MAYA ANGELOU (1928 - 2014)

Maya Angelou, known primarily for her poetry, is truly a renaissance woman who has done it all. Born Marguerite Ann Johnson, she was raised by her grandmother because her parents had abandoned her and her brother at a very young age. The presence of a loving grandmother instilled a spirit of kindness in her from childhood that she passed down to her children, grandchildren, and great-grandchildren. Like her grandmother before her, she is living proof that grandmothers make a world of difference in the lives they touch.

ARETHA FRANKLIN (1942 - 2018)

This powerhouse singer was raised in the church. After her parent's divorce and her mother's premature death, she became a young mother at 15. Luckily for her, her grandmother raised her son so that she could continue her budding career. Aretha was allowed to live to realize her dream earning eighteen Grammy's because of her grandmother.

RUTH BELL GRAHAM (1920 - 2007)

Ruth McCue Bell was born in China as the daughter of medical missionaries. Her confession of faith caused her to vow never to marry. She later reneged on this vow, accepting the proposal of a young evangelist named Billy Graham. Though she was unconventional in her ways, she raised five children and witnessed the wonder of nineteen grandchildren. Her sincerity, encouragement, and support not only kept her husband on track but touched many of the lives she crossed. True love was what she had to give, and love was all that was needed from those that loved her.

JOYCE MEYER (1943 -)

Joyce Meyer is a household name in most Christian homes. Although she is the mother of four and grandmother to ten, little is said about her life as a grandmother. Yet, on top of heading a successful ministry, she leaves quite an impression on the generations to come. Her breakout book, Every Which Way to Pray, is the beginning of sharing the simplicities of prayer, faith, and peace as the building blocks of a future that can change the lives of others.

NAOMI – A BIBLICAL EXAMPLE OF A SEASONED WOMAN

Naomi (meaning "blessed by God") is not known as a grandmother in the Bible. Yet, she had no biological grandchildren of her own. But the Bible assures us that her heart was not empty of such a joy.

In the Bible, Naomi is an example of God's restorative power. As an obedient woman, she followed her husband into the foreign land of Moab. Naomi lived there caring for her family as a supportive wife and a devoted mother.

The scripture records that her husband Elimelech died. Naomi, now a widow, was cared for by her two sons, Mahlon and Kilion, who married Moabite women. But her life took a dark turn when her sons died, leaving her alone without someone to provide for her or their widows.

Nearly destitute, Naomi decided to return to the land of Israel. With her two daughters-in-law standing before her in sadness and bitterness, she instructed them to return to their homes under the covering of their families. She was prepared to go home alone, without the covering of a husband or sons to care for her. And according to the customs and laws of Israel, Naomi was without the hope of a linage since her sons died without leaving grandchildren to whom she could pass on her values and ardent faith. Such a fate was a source of great grief in her culture.

To her, a truth that brought great grief in that culture.

One daughter-in-law chose to stay with her relatives in Moab, but Ruth clung to Naomi. Naomi's influence as a seasoned woman of faith had captured Ruth's heart, and Ruth vowed that she would go wherever Naomi chose to go.

Even with the heaviness of heart that Naomi carried, she and Ruth made the journey and finally settled in the land of Israel. Naomi mentored Ruth, instructing her and instilling her with knowledge and wisdom.

Ruth took it upon herself to provide for Naomi. She followed the custom in which women would follow the harvesters and glean the leftover wheat from the nearby fields. Being a stranger there, Ruth stayed back behind the other women and gathered what even the other women left behind.

In time, as you read the book of Ruth, we learn that the owner of the field took notice of Ruth. His name was Boaz, and he was a kinsman of Elimelech and Naomi's sons. So, in the weeks and months that followed, under the wise counsel of Naomi, Ruth made herself known to Boaz and told him that she was Naomi's daughter-in-law.

In time, Boaz took Ruth to be his wife, and she bore a son.

The significance of this can be found in Deuteronomy 25:5-6:

> If brethren dwell together and one of them dies, and have no child, the wife of the dead shall not marry without unto a stranger: her husband's brother shall go in unto her, and take her to him as wife, and perform the duty of an husband's brother unto her. And it shall be, that the firstborn which she beareth shall succeed in the name of his brother which is dead, that his name be not put out of Israel.

By Jewish law, Boaz was known as a "Redeemer Kinsman" because he had taken the wife of one of his relatives who had died without an heir. In this way, Naomi was provided a grandchild. Boaz with Ruth restored Naomi's sense of worth and purpose. In Ruth 4:16-17, we read:

> Then Naomi took the child and laid him on her bosom, and
> became a nurse to him. Also, the neighbor women gave him
> a name, saying, "There is a son born to Naomi." And they
> called his name Obed. He is the father of Jesse, the father of
> David.

Once destined to be forgotten, Naomi's name is enshrined as the great-great-grandmother of David, the King of Israel through whose linage came the Christ, Savior of the World.

And at the heart of this story, we find a seasoned woman who faced the trials of her life with great grace and a nurturing spirit to the only person left in her life, Ruth, whose story has inspired millions for generations - Ruth 4:13-17.

EPILOGUE

This book came to be for an extraordinary reason.

I could not allow the future generations of our family to barely know about their great-great-grandmother, nor be unaware of how pivotal her life was to those of us who followed her. Her stories, beliefs, desires are part of their history and should not go untold.

As a Seasoned GEM myself, I hope my short story will encourage you to share a little about your family with the young people around you. Whether they know it or not, they need us.

We who mentor must continue to educate the minds of our young. We might be the one life-changing influence that could save others from choices that could ruin their lives, like addictions or unwanted pregnancies. Collectively, we can inspire our youth to value themselves, pursue an education, make choices to enhance their personal development, and ultimately be transformed by following the ways of God.

First, kick off the "rocking chair" mindset. It is not time to stop and rest yet. We have work to do. We have plenty to give. John 9:4 reminds us that we "must work the works of him that sent me, while it is day: the night cometh, when no man can work." So, we shall pass our wisdom forward to build up and provide direction for the young women we encounter daily.

Secondly, a young woman or girl is suffering with no one to guide them, waiting for someone to mentor them. They may not have grandparents to make them aware of their personal histories, no one to share their stories.

Let's work together to reach them and help them build their stories. We need to urge them through encouraging words, developing a hunger to educate their minds, and motivating them toward a life that uses their God-given gifts and talents.

Thirdly, while we as grandmothers and seasoned women wear many hats, perhaps the most important is the role of storyteller, sharing our own stories and values with our grandchildren. Of course, not every story is perfect. But we must share our stories, imperfect as they may be, because our stories helped make us the people we are today.

My background with my Mimi was as close to perfect as any child could imagine. When it came to making some decisions on my own, it was not all perfect; everything was not a bed of roses. However, I am a child of God, a blessed grandmother, mother of two beautiful children, a minister of the Gospel, and an entrepreneur. My story did not end at the point of my greatest weaknesses but with the faith that emerged from the influence of my GEMs.

I feel that Christian grandmothers and seasoned women have a role to portray in helping our families and the extended family in the Body of Christ. Even if you do not have any grandchildren, you are still a seasoned woman. Reach out to help the younger women who are in your paths.

The Bible clearly states in Titus 2:4 that the older women are to help the younger ones. For example, my grandmother became my model with her kindness, but she did not stop with me. She spoiled my friends, also. They loved her; they enjoyed when she would cook and pass out treats. She set the bar high; her loving, unselfish example has transformed the lives of those she touched. She exemplified the character of Christ.

As a Christian GEM, I hope to inspire an awakening in your spirit. We are the next generation's teachers; let us tell our story well so that we can finish strong. Write a book that will tell your history; share your fortunes, failures, progresses, and pitfalls. Every part of your story has a trace of grace. Share wisdom, keys of understanding that will spread down through the generations.

All our stories collectively are ageless. We all form a circle of prominence and promise in society, and we all are here for a reason. None of us leave here without leaving our mark. Let's not aim for sitting in our rocking chair just yet; more work is to be done. Everything we share can be lessons learned by someone else. Regardless of our age, we can all say that the Lord has blessed us with immeasurable favor and is ever ready to infuse us with His wise counsel.

Consider the following scripture from The Message Bible:

Live Well, Live Wisely

> Do you want to be counted wise, to build a reputation for wisdom? Here's what you do: Live well, live wisely, live humbly. It's the way you live, not the way you talk, that counts. Mean-spirited ambition isn't wisdom. Boasting that you are wise isn't wisdom. Twisting the truth to make you sound wise isn't wisdom. It's the furthest thing from wisdom—it's animal cunning, devilish conniving. Whenever you're trying to look better than others or get the better of others, things fall apart, and everyone ends up at the others' throats
>
> — JAMES 3:13-16, MSG

Maintain humility and continually practice wisdom. Through prayer, knowledge, wisdom, influence, and ability are gained. Moreover, the products of prayer provide us the power to affect change within ourselves and in the hearts and lives of others.

We have the voice of experience that enables us to reach others and promote growth within our homes and communities.

God has blessed us with the maturity to jump hurdles of failures with grace, style, class, and finesse. We stand here today, alive with grace and strength.

I also remember a quote from the Christian writer Max Lucado:

A woman's heart should be so hidden in God that a man has to seek Him to find her.

As seasoned women, we should aspire to such a life. A seasoned woman's heart is a precious diamond, a priceless GEM hidden within as well as emerging from her relationship with her Savior.

If you are reading this paragraph, you have achieved a significant milestone. You have begun an ecliptic transformation from uncertainty to a life of direction and awareness of your purpose in this world. Yet, as must not forget, we are not of this world. So, I leave you with this final thought that should become ingrained in the marrow of the bones of every woman who chooses to embrace this continuing journey:

> Finally, we may note that the modern concept of "retirement" is unknown in the Bible. The Levites retired from official service at age fifty, but they then assisted younger priests - Numbers 8:24-26). In the New Testament period, Zechariah considered himself old, but he continued his service in the temple - Luke 1:18-25. Without a doubt, in ancient agricultural societies, the nature of physical labor meant cessation from work at a relatively early age. But retirees were

then responsible for training their grandchildren and became advisors for the younger generation. The Bible has no concept of ending one's life-work in order to spend the remainder of one's days in leisure.

— WILLIAM T. ARNOLD

The aged women likewise, that they be in behavior as
    becometh holiness, not false accusers, not given to much
    wine, teachers of good things; That they may teach the
    young women to be sober, to love their husbands, to love
    their children, To be discreet, chaste, keepers at home, good,
    obedient to their own husbands, that the word of God be
    not blasphemed

— TITUS 2:3-5

LEARNING GOD THROUGH SELF-TRANSFORMATION NOW!

Transform my mind
Posture my thinking toward success
I am part of a winner's circle
I am an achiever
I will not be afraid of what or who lies ahead of me
I will not walk as a failure
Failure will not defeat me
Failure will not determine my destiny
Giving up is not an option
I may have been down, but don't count me out

Transformation now!
Fear will not overtake me
Fear will not mentally destroy my dreams
Fear of rejection get out of my way
I will not speak words that destroy my future
I refuse to talk weak, walk feeble, or hide in a corner in defeat

Transformation now!
I will not walk with hunched over shoulders
I will straighten my back
Lift my head high
Pick myself up from my past failures
Dust myself off and move forward

I speak Transformation now!
Hidden potential is all in me
I have broken free of past bondages
I have the attitude of a conqueror
The chains have been broken off my mind

I am breaking out of the box that I have allowed myself to
     climb into or allowed others to put me in

I have power to profess, possess, progress, and perform
I speak to myself to my inner conscience
Awake now!
Emerge now!
Transition now!
Transform now!
My mind is strong
My path is sure
My destiny is promised
I am transformed by the renewing of my mind!
When? Here and now!
Watch Out World
Here I Come
Failures I serve you notice
I'm here now!

— AUTHOR TONI KLECKLEY

The more we believe in God and love God, the more love we have for
ourselves. Therefore, knowing God is the path to discovering myself
as the child born of His transformational grace. The relationship
defines a life of faith.

Ye are of God, little children, and have overcome them: because
     greater is He that is in you, than he that is in the world.

— I JOHN 4:4

God Bless You!

REFERENCES

American Grandparents Association (2016) Retrieved from: http://www.grandparents.com/food-and-leisure/celebrity/maya-angelou-words

Baker's Evangelical Dictionary Study Light (1987) Bibliography J.G. Harris, Biblical Perspectives on Aging: God and the Elderly, R.K. Harrison

Barharin, O (2002) Retrieved from: http://www.d.umn.edu/-balbert/documents/CharacteristicsofAfricanFamilies.pdf

Billy Graham Evangelistic Association from: http://billygraham.org/decision-magazine/june-2013/ruth-bell-graham-a-life-well-lived/

Biography (2014) Retrieved from: https://www.biography.com/video/aretha-franklin-mini-biography-2079133881

Catholic Education (2014) Retrieved from: http://catholiceducation.org/articles/marriage/mf0032.html

Chandler, D. (2013) Retrieved from: http://newsone.com/2089258/soujourner-truth-biography/http://www.poetryfoundation.org/bio/nikki-giovanni

Christian Post (2013) Retrieved from: http://www.christianpost.com/news/joyce-meyer-debuts-childrens-book-every-which-way-to-pray-71911/

Driscoll, M. (2010) Retrieved from: http://marshill.se.marshill/2010/10/13/this-is-how-we-define-church

Grandparents (2016) Retrieved from: http://www.grandparents.com/food-and-leisure/celebrity/maya-angelou-words

NewsOne (2012) Retrieved from: http://newsone.com/208258/sojourner-truth-biography/

Walter Bauer-Frederick Dunker (2000) A Greek-English Lexicon of the New Testament and Other Early Christian Literature.

*Bibliography. J. G. Harris, Biblical Perspectives on Aging: God and the Elderly; R. K. Harrison, ISBE, 3:587.

COMMUNITY RESOURCES

THE KINSHIP PROGRAM OF FRANKLIN COUNTY

GEM is a proud member and dedicated supporter in good standing with the Kinship Program of Franklin County.

Kingship Care refers to a temporary or permanent arrangement in a relative or any non-relative adult who has a long-standing relationship or bond with the child and family, has taken over the full-time, substitute care of a child whose parents are unable or unwilling to do so. This includes those relationships established through an informal arrangement, legal custody, or guardianship order, a relative foster care placement, or kinship adoption.

Regardless of the type of kinship care arrangement, the kinship caregivers' voluntary commitment to devote their lives to the children in their care is a courageous, life-changing decision.

For more information, please contact them at:

4200 E. Fifth Ave. 2nd Floor
Columbus, Ohio 43219
Telephone Help Desk: (866) 886-3537, option 4
Main Office Line: (614) 466-4359

OHIO GRANDPARENTS KINSHIP COALITION

Ohio Grandparents Kinship Coalition (OGKC) consists of kinship caregivers, advocates, and agencies throughout Ohio. The OGKC is a statewide organization that provides information and networking for caregivers taking care of children other than their own when the parents are unwilling or unable to care for them.

For more information, please get in touch with OGKC at info@ohiograndparentkinship.org

WOMEN'S EMPOWERMENT CENTER FOR ENTREPRENEURS

THE FINANCIAL WOMEN'S ASSOCIATION

The Financial Women's Association brings together high-achieving professionals from every sector of the financial world. We are dedicated future leaders, enhancing the role of women in finance and investing in the community. We are dedicated future leaders, enhancing the role of women in finance and investing in the community. In this vital work, we are fortunate to partner with prestigious institutions, government agencies, and talented individuals.

WOMEN'S BUSINESS CENTER OF OHIO
1611 Old Leonard Ave.
Columbus, Ohio 43219
(614) 732-0981

CHOICES FOR HEALING OF THE SOUL

Choices Women's Emergency Shelter
Provides housing for women and children who are victims of
domestic violence.
Columbus, OH 43206
(614) 224-4663

Family Promise of Delaware County Temporary Family Shelter
Delaware, OH 43015
21.85 miles from the center of the city
Columbus, OH
(740) 362-7817

Franklin County Children's Services Kinship Program
Please call the 24-hour Child Abuse Hotline at (614) 229-7000 or visit
the offices of Intake & Investigations at 4071 E. Main St. Whitehall,
OH 43123

Violence Crisis Information Line

(614) 244-HOME (4641)

HUMAN TRAFFICKING

Central Ohio Rescue and Restore Coalition

The mission of CORRC (core-see) is to provide a collaborative community response to human trafficking in central Ohio through education, services, advocacy, and prosecution. To report a tip or get help, call 614 285-4357 (HELP). If you are not in Ohio, please contact the National Hotline at 1-888-888-3737.

MEET THE AUTHOR

Toni Kleckley serves as a Chaplain and Founder of Transformation Now, Inc., a 501c3 organization located in Brice, Ohio.

She considers her late grandmother to be one of the most important role models in her life, along with her anointed husband, Elder Mathis Kleckley.

Toni is an ordained and licensed minister with over 30 years in ministry. She holds a Bachelor of Arts and a Master of Arts in Pastoral Care and Counseling from Ohio Christian University and a Doctorate in Theology. Dr. Kleckley is the co-founder of the Covenant of Faith Ministry, a community outreach organization located in Columbus, Ohio.

A devoted wife, mother, and grandmother graciously views each member of her family as a gift from God; Elder Mathis and Dr. Kleckley have two adult children and are blessed with six grandchildren.

Toni strongly believes: "Within all women are grand ideas, grand purposes, and grand goals. They are developed throughout their lives. My greatest desire for Grandmother's Educating Minds (GEMs): The Mentorship and Legacy of the Seasoned Woman is that we can amass a great deal of wisdom as time goes by and we grow older. We go through seasons of error, hardship, trial, and triumph. Armed with these attributes, our biblical and moral obligation is to impart these precepts to the young women who will come after us. It is my prayer now that you have read this book, you have discovered the confidence that was always deep inside of you and becoming the GEM you were always destined to be."

More than anything else, Toni treasures her relationship with the Lord and is committed to a life of service in His will.

facebook.com/toni.kleckley

www.ingramcontent.com/pod-product-compliance
Lightning Source LLC
Chambersburg PA
CBHW060310130626
46546CB00015B/917